Peace: A Very Short Introduction

VERY SHORT INTRODUCTIONS are for anyone wanting a stimulating and accessible way into a new subject. They are written by experts, and have been translated into more than 45 different languages.

The series began in 1995, and now covers a wide variety of topics in every discipline. The VSI library currently contains over 700 volumes—a Very Short Introduction to everything from Psychology and Philosophy of Science to American History and Relativity—and continues to grow in every subject area.

Very Short Introductions available now:

Oliver P. Richmond

PEACE

A Very Short Introduction

SECOND EDITION

OXFORD
UNIVERSITY PRESS

Great Clarendon Street, Oxford, OX2 6DP,
United Kingdom

Oxford University Press is a department of the University of Oxford.
It furthers the University's objective of excellence in research, scholarship,
and education by publishing worldwide. Oxford is a registered trade mark of
Oxford University Press in the UK and in certain other countries

First edition published 2014
This edition published 2023

Impression: 1

Published in the United States of America by Oxford University Press
198 Madison Avenue, New York, NY 10016, United States of America

British Library Cataloguing in Publication Data
Data available

Library of Congress Control Number: 2022944947

ISBN 978-0-19-285702-6

Printed and bound by
CPI Group (UK) Ltd, Croydon, CR0 4YY

Contents

Acknowledgements

Thanks to Mike Pugh, Alison Watson, Lucy and Carmel Richmond, and Jasmin Ramovic for their intellectual and editorial assistance, as well as several anonymous reviewers. Thanks also to my colleagues formerly at the University of St Andrews, presently at the University of Manchester, as well as the many institutions around the world where I have been lucky enough to discuss my work. Thanks, finally, to Sandra and Leander for providing the conditions to make this book possible.

List of illustrations

Chapter 1
The multiple dimensions of peace

A sketch

The story of peace is as old as the story of humanity itself, and certainly as old as war. It is a story of terrible setbacks—as with the Russian invasion of Ukraine in 2022—and progress—as might be seen in varying degrees in countries like Colombia, or in Northern Ireland, in the Balkans, or Timor-Leste. Peace is always made in very difficult circumstances, as this volume will illustrate. Historically, peace has often been taken, as with the *Oxford English Dictionary*'s definition, to imply an absence of overt violence or war between or sometimes within states. War is often thought to be the natural state of humanity, peace of any sort being fragile and fleeting. This book challenges this view. Peace in its various forms has been by far humanity's objective—as the archaeological, ethnographic, and historic records indicate. Peace has left a historical legacy, a series of sedimental layers, institutional frameworks, methods, and tools aimed at preventing war. Frameworks for security, law, redistribution of resources, representation, reconciliation, and justice have constantly been advancing as can be seen in the United Nations' recent 'Sustaining Peace' agenda (2016).

Yet, despite such developments, international relations remain subject to a range of geopolitical tensions, and the failure of a range of peacebuilding, peacekeeping, and mediation tools, as in Libya, Yemen, and Syria. Many of the peacekeeping and peacemaking processes, in places such as the Middle East, the Democratic Republic of Congo, or Cyprus, are now frozen into the political landscape, and have been so for decades. In ongoing conflicts, as with Russia's invasion in Ukraine, the tools of peacekeeping, peacemaking, and peacebuilding are slow to be engaged, seem to be very limited, and reactive. After so much promise in the latter part of the 20th century, what has gone wrong and what should be done?

The earliest classical thinkers, including the Sophists, Plato (*c*.428–348 BC), Aristotle (384–322 BC), to Cicero (106–43 BC) and later Augustine (AD 354–430), debated how virtuous and peaceful political order could be designed, as well as the pros and cons of the relationship between war and politics, as in Thucydides' contribution (*c*.460–*c*.400 BC). The question of the span of political community was crucial even at this early point: was it a matter of territory, a language group, or simply existing in the world—a citizen of the world, as the Stoic Diogenes the Cynic (*c*.412–323 BC) argued, followed by Seneca (*c*.4 BC–AD 65) and Plutarch (*c*.AD 46–119)? Other thinkers such as Marcus Aurelius (AD 121–80) also favoured trying to understand other communities and peoples.

During its long evolution since such classical engagements, peace came to be organized domestically within the state, internationally through global organizations and institutions, or transnationally through actors whose ambit covers all of these levels. After the Enlightenment, world government, federation, or confederation came to represent a global constitutional dream, debated by the Duc de Sully (1560–1641), with his 'Grand Design' in the 17th century, and by Kant (1724–1804), Rousseau (1712–78), Bentham (1748–1832), and others. The reality of the current international system is that it has evolved into something far more complex and far less elegant than Kant envisioned.

Peace can be public or private, politically organized to balance great power interests or sociologically constructed to maintain peace and order in everyday life. Peace at this level has often been a hidden phenomenon, subservient to power and interests.

Peace practices and theories have made huge advances throughout history. However, violence remains a political or economic tool. It does not help that peace is a rather ambiguous concept. Authoritarian governments and powerful states have, throughout history, had a tendency to impose their version of peace on their own citizens as well as those of other states, as with the Soviet Union's suppression of dissent amongst its own population and those of its satellite states, such as East Germany or Czechoslovakia. Peace and war may be closely connected, such as when military force is deployed to force peace, as with North Atlantic Treaty Organization (NATO) airstrikes in Bosnia-Herzegovina in 1995 and in Kosovo in 1999.

Over the last 300 years or so an international peace architecture (IPA) has come into existence. It represents several sedimental layers including formal and informal systems designed to prevent various types of war and build a better political order. They have been essential for the survival of all political orders, from city-states, to empires, as well as the modern states system. The IPA spans great power diplomacy, a balance of power framework, international law, multilateralism, and organizational frameworks such as the United Nations (UN), the European Union (EU), NATO, the African Union (AU), and many others. It includes tools for international peacekeeping and mediation, arbitration, disarmament, constitutional reform, development, and democratization. It has included social mobilization to expand and claim new rights and security. It has been supported by global civil society networks. It represents an inter-generational effort to overcome war, but it has also tended to be reactive, fragile, and has often failed to stop war. Indeed, it is geared to prevent or end the last type of war, rather than the next, violence being a

3

fast-evolving phenomenon. However, over the longer term, it has become more complex and adept, culminating in the international system of diplomacy, law, and treaties, the UN system, donor networks, development frameworks, and global civil society.

A wide range of sources representing a broader scientific and historical agreement indicate that the emergence of peace is closely associated with a variety of political, social, economic, and cultural struggles against war and oppression. Many of the innovations in peacemaking and its consolidation first emerged in such struggles. Peace activism has normally been based on campaigns for individual and group rights and needs, for material and legal equality between groups, genders, races, and religions, disarmament, and to build international institutions to govern the behaviour of states, militaries, and empires. This has in the long term required the construction of local and international associations, networks, and institutions, which coalesced around widely accepted agendas. Peace activism supported internationally organized civil society campaigns against slavery in the 18th century, workers' rights, enfranchisement, equality, and for basic human dignity and rights ever since. Various peace movements struggled against imperial or occupying states for decolonization, independence, and self-determination, or for voting rights and disarmament (most famously perhaps, the Campaign for Nuclear Disarmament). Ordinary people can, and have often, mobilized for peace in societal terms using peaceful methods of resistance (as with Indian non-violent opposition to British rule in the 1920s until Independence in 1947).

Despite such wide-ranging advances, there remains controversy over whether peace or war is humanity's 'natural condition'. The political left claims there is a constant struggle against oppression and hegemony to achieve justice and peace, and that only a broad version of peace is acceptable, often requiring international collaboration. Conversely, the right claims that violence is endemic and inherent in human society and so a narrow version is the only

4

pragmatic choice for the state. A 'Leviathan' is often needed, which is focused on national interests that normally preclude international cooperation to any significant degree.

In addition to the contestation over a minimalist or maximalist version of peace, there is also the glaring question as to whether war and violence are, directly or indirectly, profitable for states or those actors engaged in them. Much scientific thought agrees that social, political, and economic inequality in society, as well as in the international system, which have often been taken to represent natural stratifications, are important sources of power and rent for key actors in the international political economy. It might be simplistic to say that inequality and injustice are thus also causes for war, especially as they are carried down across generations, but it is also very plausible as a systemic explanation. Thus, blockages in peace processes, whether relating to spoilers or incompatible interests, may be forms of organized opposition to peace—in other words, a counter-peace process. There may also be systemic, structural forms of counter-peace. This dynamic, little remarked upon, follows the pattern of counter-revolutions, which have often, in a Burkean sense, tried to reverse the emancipatory gains of revolutions such as the French or American in the 18th century (in his case to preserve the interests of the aristocracy). Blockages may emerge from the policies of governments intent on the national interest or the defence of a people's historical privilege as well as from actors, warlords, insurgents who have broken the prohibition of the use of violence in the political terrain. It also reflects the counter-insurgency strategies that dominant actors often used in colonial history to put down popular insurgencies, which were often aimed at self-determination and the hope of overturning economic exploitation.

This short book outlines the positive, though complex and often controversial, story of the evolution of peace in practice and theory (mainly from the perspective of the global north). It should be noted that non-Western peace traditions, spanning the major historical civilizations, religions, and identities, now also play a substantial role in these debates. The West has been the loudest and most influential voice—for better or worse—in defining the politics and economics of peace since the Enlightenment, even despite the resurgence of the global south after formal decolonization or the rise of China. It has promoted the 'liberal peace', upon which the post-Second World War and post-Cold War IPA has been based. Since the early 2000s, this framework has looked incredibly fragile, however. The search continues for better alternatives or refinements.

Chapter 2
Defining peace

Defining peace and its dimensions is a difficult task. There is no single definition. A starting point is to think either in terms of a narrow version, which implies the ending of open violence without resolving its underlying causes, or a broader version, which implies liberal peace or peace with justice. The current situation in Cyprus where Greek and Turkish Cypriot military forces, or Korea where North and South Korean forces confront each other daily across a demilitarized line might be described as a negative peace, as would the failed peace treaty after the First World War (The Treaty of Versailles). By contrast a broad version would produce a peace agreement, peaceful state, society, and regional order, perhaps according to a single universal model of positive peace, as Johan Galtung (1930–) argued. The European Union's emergence from the ruins of the Second World War is an example. It has the ambition of dealing with underlying, structural violence. In a further step, multiple versions of peace (a hybrid peace framework) would imply coexistence of very different social and political systems. The peace agreement between Egypt and Israel in 1978 is an example of this approach, in which very different states and peoples with many remaining and deep disagreements came to a limited agreement. Another, more recent example is offered by the hybrid form of peace that is emerging in Timor-Leste since the Indonesian occupation ended in 1999.

Each of these versions of peace offers different levels of security and rights for society: a narrow version would be basic and stable for as long as power relations remained unchanged; a broader version more complex but also more just, and a hybrid approach even more complex, more just, but perhaps less stable because of its complexity. Underlying each type is a central question: does one make peace by subjugating one's enemies, assimilating them, or by accepting, and thus becoming reconciled to their differences?

Negative peace

A narrow understanding of peace indicates an absence of overt violence (such as warfare or low-intensity conflict) both between and within states. This may take the form of a ceasefire, a power-sharing agreement, or exist within an authoritarian political system. It indicates that one state, or group in society, dominates another through violence or more subtle means (no peace, no war, in other words). This approach has the benefit of simplicity, but will always be fragile because it is based on ever-shifting configurations of power. Hidden structural and cultural violence embedded in social, economic, and political systems remains unaddressed. This might explain why, after various ceasefires in the 2000s, the peace process collapsed in Colombia on several occasions. The core issues of the dispute, in particular relating to land distribution, poverty, and socio-economic inequality, have not as yet been addressed. A peace agreement based on a narrow understanding of peace would probably not be satisfactory in anything other than the short term. Military force or an authoritarian government may maintain a basic security order—as in East Germany during the Cold War—but many deficits relating to human rights, democratic representation, justice, and prosperity remain as markers of structural violence.

negative understanding of peace draws on an 'inherency' view
that violence is intrinsic to human nature, and is endemic in
society, history, and amongst states. Such an argument is often
drawn from observations of how animals appear to behave,
particularly primates (though the applicability of such evidence is
much disputed). If conflict is endemic because it is rooted in
human nature then little can be done about it other than by using
force to promote strategic interests. Security in these terms means
the preservation of a pre-existing hierarchy of states, their
territorial sovereignty, and a balance of power between them—as
in 19th-century Europe and the 'Concert System' post-1815. This
was the attitude toward war and conflict and their relationship
with a negative peace from ancient times until at least the
Enlightenment, perhaps until the emergence of fascism in the
early 20th century. Peace existed (somewhat conveniently for, and
from, the perspective of kings, queens, emperors, and various
dictators) mainly as a painful stalemate between rulers, or
absolute victory, in between the frequent wars that took place
across history. In this history, human beings are merely pawns of
the powerful and their interests.

Positive peace

Such views were slowly supplanted by positive peace approaches
after the Enlightenment. A broader understanding of peace
indicates both the lack of open violence between and within states,
and the aim of creating the conditions for society to live without
fear or poverty, within a broadly agreed political system
(i.e. responding to structural, cultural, and environmental violence).
It implies the relative fulfilment of individuals in society, as well as
stable political institutions, law, economics, states, and regions.
It represents the proverbial 'good life' or the 'Perpetual Peace'
to which famous philosophers from Aristotle (384–322 BC) to
Immanuel Kant (1724–1804), a German liberal philosopher, have
often alluded. Much of post-Enlightenment political history,
especially since the Treaty of Westphalia in 1648, reflects an

attempt to develop a scientific conceptualization of peace in positive terms as a response to Europe's incessant wars by building an IPA.

Indeed, it is possible to claim that in fact peacemaking has been one of the most common activity of humanity in history. As every society has experienced conflict on various levels, all societies have developed sophisticated methods for peacemaking—from social institutions to formal legal processes and public institutions. Conflict and war are learned behaviours that can be prevented or mitigated through tools such as military intervention (ironically), diplomacy, compromise, agreement, redistribution of resources, and education.

This view has shaped the attempt during the 20th century to build a positive peace, defined as long-term stability, sustainability, and social justice. From this understanding developed the post-war League of Nations Mandate (1920) and the UN system (1945). It also led to tools such as mediation, as used by US President Carter after the 1974 war in the Middle East between Egypt and Israel, peacekeeping as in Cyprus, Congo, and many other countries, conflict resolution and transformation now widely used at the civil society level, and peacebuilding as used from Cambodia to Bosnia-Herzegovina in the 1990s.

A public or official narrative of history tends to be dominated by elites (kings, queens, emperors, politicians, the military, religious figures, the very rich, and, more often, Western or Northern men). However, there is also a private transcript of everyday history that offers a more nuanced understanding of human history and society. In this private transcript, a positive peace is located in everyday life. This social peacemaking tendency may be less visible than the ruptures caused by violence but nonetheless it contributes to the development of political and international institutions—from local governance, national parliaments, and the UN system.

sitive peace approaches have also engendered a shift from aditional notions of security where the onus was on the state to ecure its territory and sovereignty, as Max Weber (1864–1920) argued. This view has been nuanced by a version of security where human beings, rather than the state, are the main focus. A positive peace, along with concepts such as 'human security' (which in 1994 was defined by a UN Development Programme official as 'freedom from fear, freedom from want') rests upon arguments that violence is learned rather than innate in society so conflict may be mutually and consensually resolved. Direct, cultural, and structural violence can be removed, offering a form of peace as an outcome of political reform, akin to the everyday lives that many people experience in developed liberal democracies. This means security, law, order, and prosperity have become comparatively and relatively routine in post-war settlements, as happened for many European countries after the Second World War. Under such conditions social justice (human rights, democratic representation, relative material equality, and prosperity), the accountability of states and elites, as well as peace between states, may be achieved.

A positive peace approach maintains that conflict can be resolved fully by people, states, and institutions through a range of innovative responses. These might lead to local, everyday, as well as transnational or international peace campaigns, institutions, and architectures. As well as addressing social, economic, political, military, and resource dynamics of conflict, positive peace also engages with identity, class, race, gender, labour, and ethnic differences. Such multiple and entwined causes require multi-disciplinary, multidimensional, and sophisticated responses, if conflict is to be resolved.

The concept of a positive peace has been significant in policy terms. It has influenced how conflict is understood and addressed by states and by various international or regional organizations: the UN, World Bank, and international donors or governments, especially those of the OECD and G20, as well as the European Union.

Everyday and hybrid peace

A further sophistication indicates that there exist multiple conceptions of peace across the range of cultures, states, and societies around the world. Most societies, however 'modern' or 'traditional', have their own version of everyday peace, drawn from custom, social, and other context-dependent factions, which is eventually scaled up into a political order. These often engender different, or at least nuanced, notions of social harmony, economic prosperity, political institutions, and law, as well as respect for historical traditions and identity. Enabling coexistence between different entities practising different forms of peace would require mediation between them and cooperation at the social, state, and international level. However peace is defined, it has always attracted innovative or radical thought, action, and has led to hybridized institutions and practices, aimed at defining peace through justice rather than by power.

Theory and practice

The entire history of peace in Western and often 'Eurocentric' thought spans the thought of the ancient Greek philosopher Plato to the emergence of NATO after the Second World War, the recent history of non-governmental organization and networks, multilateralism and regional integration, and attempts to develop reconciliation based upon cooperation between former enemies. Over the years of its existence, the UN (often through the General Assembly or its many agencies) has compiled and released documents, reports, and resolutions, outlining innovations in the field and drawing on a wide global consensus. These have offered platforms for doctrines and strategies designed to deal with the complicated relationship between power and peace: from its programmes for 'cultures of peace'; rights to peace; on the need

new economic orders'; economic, social, and cultural rights; to
dependence, self-determination, development, and
peacebuilding. Most recently, the UN's 'Sustaining Peace' agenda
2018) has emerged which reiterates the connection of peace with
justice and sustainability.

Reflecting positive, everyday peace approaches, these
contributions have called for equality in identity and gender
terms, self-determination, participation, cooperation, social
justice, and development. They have endorsed a right to culture,
society, and work, and to choose one's own identity. They have
called for an international states-system framed in the interests of
peace, justice, and sustainability. Representatives of much of the
planet's population signed these documents, yet such global
political and scientific consensus has been easily ignored. Thus,
the evolution of peace has been slow, and rather than a single,
positive, universal peace emerging, this process appears to be
leading to an interlocking system of hybrid and multiple 'peaces'.
By the 2020s this phenomena reflected an increasingly multi-polar
(as opposed to multilateral) international environment.

In the contemporary era, more active concepts such as
'peacebuilding', 'development', 'conflict resolution', 'conflict
transformation', 'statebuilding', and 'stabilization' are often used
interchangeably with the word 'peace'. Within the UN system
policymakers generally agree that they should try to address the
root causes of conflict.

Several important lines of thought converge in modern theoretical
approaches to peace: one focused on the constitution of the state,
another on the role of international organizations, another on the
underlying philosophy of peace, and another on peace movements
emerging from society.

Peace thinking also has long had religious connotations, arising
from the way different religions treat violence and promote

tolerance throughout history. Such views span concepts such a
'just war', self-defence, non-violence, civil society, human rights,
liberal democracy, liberal internationalism, the democratic peace
coexistence, and pacifism (drawing on Christian, Confucian,
Buddhist, and Hindu philosophy).

Some general theories, dynamics, and themes prominent in the
historical discussion of peace reappear in its theories. The
best-known approach in political theory is called *political realism*.
Early contributors included authors such as Sun Tzu (an ancient
Chinese military strategist and philosopher who was the author of
The Art of War in the 5th century BC), Thucydides (an ancient
Greek historian from the 5th century BC, who because of his
experiences in the Peloponnesian War between Sparta and Athens
claimed that power rather than morality was important in war),
and Augustine (a Latin philosopher and theologian during the late
Roman Empire in the 5th century AD). Realism mainly focuses on
the military (and later on economic) power of states, their clashes,
an attempt to understand what makes war 'just', and attempts to
produce a balance of power as the main mechanism of conflict
management.

Machiavelli, an Italian historian, politician, diplomat, and
philosopher based in Florence during the Renaissance, argued in
his famous book *The Prince*, published around 1532:

> A wise prince ought to observe some such rules, and never in
> peaceful times stand idle, but increase his resources with industry
> in such a way that they may be available to him in adversity, so that
> if fortune changes it may find him prepared to resist her blows.
>
> (chapter XIV)

Nevertheless, the common view that the ancient period was
defined by an acceptance of the inevitability of war is mistaken.
Even Machiavelli, more often associated with power and interests,

ought that elections were necessary and peace should be fair
nd voluntary.

Later, in the course of Enlightenment philosophy, Thomas
Hobbes's *Leviathan* (1588–1671, 1651) set out social contract
theory, including the need for political representation, individual
rights, and notions of civil society. Drawing on his experience of
the English civil war, Hobbes argued for a social contract between
the population and an absolute sovereign (called a Leviathan after
a biblical monster). He thought that preventing a 'war of all
against all' required a Leviathan in the form of a strong central
government.

Peace was understood in a relatively narrow way in realist
thought, in which it was defined by merely the absence of open
violence. Structural violence might remain. Key modern scholars
and policy figures in this tradition, such as Henry Kissinger (born
in 1923, a scholar and Secretary of State for Presidents Richard
Nixon and Gerald Ford), influenced by experiences in the Second
World War and during the Cold War, often saw peace mainly as a
balance of power between states. They often drew on 18th- and
19th-century European history.

There have long been challenges to political realism. An important
approach draws on ancient critiques of militarism, following those
of Confucius (a 6th-century BC Chinese philosopher), that war
would not give rise to peace. Government should focus on the
well-being of the people, not on making war. Given the legitimacy
and attractiveness of peace, it has often been central to any
civilization's narrative about its place in the world. In the case of
China, Confucius himself said that 'pacific harmony' bound society
together. He offered his famous aphorism that peace extended
from the heart to the family, then to society, and to the world.
Daoism connected inner, social, and collective harmony, which
also incidentally required a norm of non-interference. Even

during the Warring States period of Chinese history, famous voices decried war (and the realist propositions of Sun Tzu) in favour of the merits of peace. Confucius' focus on 'civil virtues' was the most famous of these: among other wise statements, he argued in his book *Analects*, '... [r]ecompense injury with justice, and recompense kindness with kindness'. His work has more recently been reclaimed as an emblem of modern China's 'peaceful development'.

Alternative approaches to realism developed early on. Respect, civil virtue, neighbourliness, cooperation, morality, trade, good governance, kinship, and treaties were motifs of early, more idealistic representations of peace. Another characteristic of early thinking on peace was the relationship with government and citizens, from Plato onwards. Peace was in the interests of a 'philosopher-king' who exercises his judgement for the good of all, however difficult this may be, according to Plato's *Republic*. In addition, in ancient Greek philosophy around the 3rd century BC, the Epicureans crystallized a growing concern with everyday conditions for ordinary people, and the Stoics rejected the passions of greed, anger, or lust, calling for self-discipline and solidarity. Even at this early stage, individuals were mobilizing for peaceful and improved political orders, realizing that their local and social environment was crucial, that peace required different types of approaches, and that it had implications for the design of the polity, as well as an international dimension.

These more idealistic approaches were associated with issues of abundance and dignity, as with the Greek goddess Eirene, who as the personification of peace was often depicted in art as a beautiful young daughter of Zeus, carrying a cornucopia. They also suggested a rejection of war and violence through various social strategies, as exemplified in Aristophanes' comic play *Lysistrata* (411 BC) in which Lysistrata persuaded women to try to end the Peloponnesian War by withholding sexual privileges in order to force men to negotiate a peace settlement.

...tually there emerged a historical build-up of diplomatic ...ce treaties over time in ancient Greece, reflecting more ...alistic as well as power-based understandings, aimed at ...reating a 'common peace'. This path was opening up for a more cosmopolitan approach.

Another contribution drew on the thinking of the Christian philosopher Augustine, known as 'just war', which effectively limited the scope of war to certain specific situations. In his book *The City of God*, Augustine wrote:

> A just war is wont to be described as one that avenges wrongs, when a nation or state has to be punished, for refusing to make amends for the wrongs inflicted by its subjects, or to restore what it has seized unjustly.

Thomas Aquinas (1225–74) later developed this in some detail. War was deemed just if it was in self-defence, punished aggression (but was not for revenge), was undertaken by the authorities, or was a last resort. It should ultimately make peace. This framework persisted in international relations, reinvented as humanitarian intervention and regime change war by the 1990s in Bosnia-Herzegovina and the 2000s in Iraq, respectively.

Modern theories of idealism and liberalism are closely related to these debates, and are often associated with Immanuel Kant and his plan for 'Perpetual Peace'. During the 17th and 18th centuries debates about peace began to coalesce into what was then termed a 'grand design' in European political thought (as mentioned in the work of the Duc de Sully between 1638 and 1662). This laid the foundations of the UN system after 1945, and might now be thought of as an international peace architecture. F. R. Hinsley (1918–98) noted in the 1960s that much of the modern architecture for peacemaking dated from the 17th century, however, implying that further updating was required (and very late).

The development of the concept of peace was enriched by Marx thinking about oppression, power and class struggle, exploitatio and revolutionary change, driven, partly at least, by grassroots actors, social movements, and their networks. This has given rise to understandings of peace that included social justice and emancipation, with important implications for the poor, women, and children. Some would argue that this has over-complicated peace in practice, however, and that the idea of violent revolutionary change, associated with some variants of Marxism, presents a conundrum for peace, in that change is essential but only non-violence is consistent with peace. Gramscian understandings of the potential of mobilization of grassroots actors for their rights have also been important.

Liberal peace and beyond

Liberal peace theory suggested that democracy ensures that domestic politics within states are peaceful. Together with free trade, international law, and organization it also ensures that states do not then go to war with each other, following the sole 'law' of international relations that democratic states do not fight each other. This argument has often been used as an explanation for the stability of Europe after the Second World War. It was also the model for the Western attempt to redevelop world order after the end of the Cold War. Though flawed it probably represents one of the most sophisticated large-scale forms in history.

The liberal peace framework can be broken down into a number of intellectual and practical traditions:

1. the **victor's peace** in which a negative peace is imposed by a victor in war;
2. the **constitutional peace** in which democracy and free trade are taken to be fundamental qualities of any peaceful state's constitution (contributing to a positive peace);

- the **institutional peace**, in which international institutions, such as the UN, international financial institutions (e.g. the Bretton Woods institutions), or state donors, act to maintain peace and order according to a mutually agreed framework of international law (contributing to a positive peace);
4. the **civil peace** tradition in which civil society organizations, NGOs, and domestic and transnational social movements seek to uncover and rectify historical injustice or processes that engender the risk of war (contributing to a positive peace).

The liberal peace has been supported by international institutions, which during the 20th century facilitated cooperation between states over problems such as disarmament and arms control and supported free trade and common norms, rules, and laws. Perhaps most importantly, it allowed for the development and spread of the concept of human rights, which created an expansionary effect around the world. When associated with peace and security, human rights underlined the contradictions of a very basic form of peace, and as with the Helsinki agreement of 1975 ('The Final Act of the Conference on Security and Cooperation in Europe', Helsinki, Finland, 1 August 1975), pointed a route towards its improvement. There has been a political, policy, and scholarly consensus around these factors, especially in the global north. In the global south, however, there was also concern that many post-colonial and developing countries were not represented fairly and had often not benefited equally from global economic conditions. This concern dated back to the 1950s and the famous Bandung Conference in 1955, which brought together newly decolonized states in order to chart a way forward for the international system that was more appropriate for developing countries (Figure 1).

Such thinking has continued to evolve with the contributions of contemporary liberal thinkers (including the American scholars

1. The Plenary Session of the Bandung Conference, 1955.

John Rawls, Michael Walzer, and Michael Doyle) and policymakers.
It connected Kant's liberal peace with broader questions of justice,
as well as the capacity to wage 'just war'. This could be seen in
doctrines like 'humanitarian intervention' (the use of force by
external actors to protect human rights) or 'regime change'
(removing a regime responsible for threats to international or
domestic peace and security), the former as in the Responsibility to
Protect Doctrine of 2005, or the latter as with US President Bush's
invasion of Iraq in 2003. Because liberal contributions argued that
peace may be legitimate if it supports the non-proliferation of
weapons, human rights, democracy, and a rule of law, a confluence
between liberal peace and intervention touched upon an old
conundrum that pacifists and revolutionaries have long faced
throughout history: is military intervention justified if it overturns
domination and ends war to bring about peace?

A range of critical and post-colonial theorists foresaw the
increasing demands made on the concept of peace. Some
highlighted the rights and needs of humanity after colonialism,

lems arising from global capitalism and neoliberalism, the
.erent biases of liberalism, and the capacity for peoples to
obilize for social justice, equality, and freedom. Among many these
included: Paulo Freire (a Brazilian philosopher (1921–97), who
wrote *Pedagogy of the Oppressed*); Frantz Fanon (a French-Algerian
writer (1925–61), whose works inspired anti-colonial liberation
movements); Homi Bhabha (a post-colonial theorist (1949–),
who showed how hybrid political frameworks arise from the
ways in which colonized peoples resist the power of the
colonizer); and Amartya Sen (an Indian economist (1933–), who
won the 1998 Nobel Memorial Prize in Economics and helped
to create the United Nations Human Development Index, which
compares and ranks each country's state of development). These
more critical views of peace sought to uncover power and its
workings and establish a fairer form of domestic and international
politics, more likely to lead to a positive, or even hybrid, form
of peace.

It is important to note a division in the contemporary
understanding of peace amongst the various schools of peace
studies around the world. Some see it as a contribution to
maintaining the dominant liberal and capitalist world order,
which for many outside the global north, however, means a
negative peace. More critical approaches see peace as connected to
global social justice and emancipation, meaning human rights,
equality, solidarity, justice, and sustainability are required. Most of
these arguments are critical of realist approaches to peace,
indicating the necessity of social justice, participatory forms of
democracy, human rights, equality, and autonomy. Some argue
that no one perspective has a monopoly on defining peace.
Multiple forms must therefore coexist, perhaps in a hybrid form of
peace. This implies that the IPA does not represent a linear,
historical development according to universal norms, but instead
a more complex, interlocking system comprising very different
types of political system.

All of these strands of thought and practice have contributed to the historical evolution of an international peace architecture. However, the current fragility of the post-Cold War order has reopened the question of what is contemporary peace? Should it follow the Western model of liberal peace or are there other alternatives, perhaps emerging from East Asia or from the contributions of the global south? In the 21st century, so far a neoliberal peace appears to have become dominant in international policy, where the focus has been on trade wars between blocs and free-market reforms. However, this approach does not meet the standards required for human rights, or everyday and hybrid dimensions, as well as sustainability or justice, as suggested in the UN's Sustaining Peace Agenda of 2018.

Chapter 3
The victor's peace in history

The victor's peace evolved from the historical view that peace emerges from a complete military victory. It is reflected in the first stage in the modern IPA, in which geopolitical power politics are moderated by strategic and diplomatic balances of peace. This form of peace was coercive and often unjust but it could be orderly, for at least as long as the victor survived to underpin it. It might even provide the basis for a more sophisticated version to emerge, though most likely only after a major breakdown in the balance of power system (as with the First World War). It has long been thought to be the oldest concept of peace, foreshadowing the Darwinian notion of the survival of the fittest and implying war and violence was humanity's natural condition.

This formulation implied military control or occupation, colonialism, or imperialism. Basic order was created through domination or alliances and a balance of power whereby states and leaders perceive war as too costly to win because of their opponent's strength. Such thinking is well described by Johann Galtung's much later formulation of a 'negative peace'.

Historical emergence

The Roman destruction of the city of Carthage (149 BC), which is in modern Tunisia, is probably the best-known and earliest example of the victor's peace. On the defeat of Carthage's armies Rome declared that the city should be razed and its lands strewn with salt, thus attempting to remove it completely from the world map. Carthage has ironically been remembered precisely for this.

A victor's peace needed more than force, however. It also needed law: the first emperor of the Babylonian empire placed stone tablets around his territories (*c*.1789 BC) outlining the terms of the peace in a 'Code of Laws', which he imposed after winning a war.

A victor's peace was discussed in a range of ancient sources. Thucydides (460–*c*.395 BC), a Greek historian and Athenian general, wrote about his experiences in his book *History of the Peloponnesian War*, between Sparta and Athens. Athens was, before the war, the most powerful city-state in Greece, but after a series of failed peace treaties with Sparta was eventually beaten. Sparta became the leading city-state in turn. The war had a devastating economic impact and undermined the idea of democracy that Athens promoted, replacing it with Sparta's authoritarian approach, and leading to repeated wars across the Hellenic world. Thucydides concluded that power determined international relations, though he also explored the problems faced by victims in the famous 'Melian Dialogue'. The Athenians stated that:

> the strong do what they can and the weak suffer what they must ... it is not as if we were the first to make this law, or to act upon it when made: we found it existing before us, and shall leave it to exist forever after us; all we do is to make use of it, knowing that you and everybody else, having the same power as we have, would do the same as we do.

A number of other historical sources laid out similar arguments and experiences. Sun Tzu, in his masterpiece of strategy *The Art of War* (5th century BC), laid out how wars could be won whilst also advocating cooperation and diplomacy with other states. The latter were also significant in Augustine's *The City of God* (5th century AD). For him war was representative of the 'fallen condition' of humanity. Nevertheless, war could be legitimately fought against the enemies of Christendom. War within Christendom was sinful, and so should be carefully conducted. The 'city of god' would be a Christian empire of peace, though it might not be peaceful in its dealings with non-Christians.

Refinement

Machiavelli's seminal study *The Prince* (1513) outlined the justifications for using immoral means to achieve glory or survival. Thomas Hobbes's *Leviathan* (1651) claimed that a 'state of nature'—meaning 'war of all against all'—could only be prevented by strong central government to which society is subservient. Abuses of power were the price of peace. These arguments grappled with the problem of which takes precedence: power, survival, or norms? Paradoxically, sometimes war was conducted for reasons of achieving peace of exclusive benefit to one or other group.

Francisco de Vitoria, a Spanish Renaissance philosopher and jurist who wrote about 'just war', thought that the stage was being set for a new era of victor's peace: uninhabited lands were available for exploitation, providing a reason for a victor's peace.

While Hobbes's *Leviathan* argued that combating of the 'state of nature' mainly rested upon the interests and capacities of the 'Leviathan' (this was a reference to a large sea monster, by which Hobbes meant a powerful actor), he was also aware of the need for consensus and legitimacy within society for any legitimate authority.

The colonial or imperial systems that arose from the power and interests of the European, industrializing states saw them take control of vast populations and swathes of land around the world

The victor's peace in history

for glory, profit, and to 'civilize the native'. This was a kind of victor's peace, based upon extraction, markets, taxation, war, and hegemony. The development of European colonialism and imperialism was predicated on the right of a 'superior' race to dominate those whom it identified as lesser.

England's exploration of new sea routes during the Elizabethan era (1558–1603) led to a rapid realization of the potential for trade, and ultimately of the financial and military benefits of territorial acquisition and control. Implicit in this development was the relationship between war, trade, and peace in the colonies and dependencies. By the end of the 19th century, European imperialism came to be characterized less by the exploitation of a territory's resources and inhabitants and more by a liberal 'civilizing mission' (which also disguised its extractive underpinnings).

Massive industrialization amplified the capacity at the disposal of states and imperial powers to make war. Some states eventually drifted towards fascism as demands grew ever greater for territory, material resources, and markets. The state was a vital component of this extreme attempt to amass power so war could be used as a political tool. According to such arguments, war might also provide a context in which individuals demonstrated their capacity for an ethical life. In fact, peace for Hegel (1770–1831), a German philosopher, would only produce a 'corruption of nations'.

The balance of power system

Given that a victor's peace was demonstrably a failure because power waxed and waned, an improvement was required, which emerged in the balance of power system that marked European politics for much of the 19th and early 20th centuries. This rested upon a system of alliances that maintained a negative peace between states and empires.

In the 19th century, after the Napoleonic Wars, the main European powers had at the Congress of Vienna in 1815 established a 'Concert' system of diplomacy aimed at balancing great power interests through diplomacy to avoid war. While rudimentary, it lasted for much of that century. It managed to mitigate geopolitical and imperial wars until it broke down at the start of the 20th century. However, it provided a geopolitical basis for future developments in creating a more sophisticated peace framework.

The weakness of such a system, as can be seen in early 20th-century European history, was that it was also susceptible to collapse. Alliances may maintain order but they may also be called upon for support against aggressive states as with Germany in 1914 and 1939. Such conflicts may quickly escalate into regional or world wars as alliance systems are triggered, and because of which the previous international system and its empires may collapse.

The outbreak of war in 1914 was greeted with a general incredulity that 'civilization' could still conduct and tolerate war. As the 'Great War's' associated direct and collateral costs mounted, it became clear that war had become an end in itself without any clear objectives or benefits. The First World War confirmed that large-scale industrialized war could not be won decisively, even at great cost. Indeed, any victor's peace might be so costly that it would be meaningless.

The Versailles Settlement followed a victor's peace, in that its terms were determined by US President Wilson's 'Fourteen Points', but it also introduced new elements. They were designed to stabilize and augment the balance of power system of the 19th century, including self-determination and democracy. Yet the settlement also left a legacy of unsolved self-determination claims. As John Maynard Keynes (1883–1946) foresaw in his book *The Economic Consequences of the Peace* (1919), the First World War's victors forced the defeated Axis powers to accept terms that might lead to war restarting in the future. This illustrated both the aim of the victor's peace—to remove the threat of the defeated forever—as well as its weaknesses—that somehow, in fact or in legend, they may rise again. As the victor's power wanes, the latter becomes more likely.

Indeed, the European empires faded swiftly from the international stage after the end of the two world wars. These wars both drained their resources and strengthened local claims for self-determination in colonies around the world.

The inter-war drift back to a victor's peace was to have a decisive effect on 20th-century history, however: not merely via its two industrial-scale world wars but more subtly on the new layers of peace architecture subsequently established after both world wars.

The creation of the League and later the UN offered the potential for new, more sophisticated advances in the practices of peacemaking but any progress was to be related to the continuing salience of geopolitics. Thus, NATO—a military alliance based on the North Atlantic Treaty of 1949—represented a collective security system designed to maintain the new order (it eventually included 28 member states across North America and Europe, and an additional 22 countries involved in NATO's 'Partnership for Peace'). NATO was politically involved in the Cold War struggle, and intervened militarily during the break-up of Yugoslavia in Bosnia in the mid-1990s and again in Kosovo in 1999, invoking a brief doctrine of humanitarian intervention. NATO also perceived the 9/11 atrocities in New York as an attack on all its members and later intervened in Afghanistan through the NATO-led International Security Assistance Force. In 2011, it enforced a no-fly zone over Libya, following UN Security Council Resolution 1973.

In these terms, any limited peace was merely an interlude until the next armed confrontation over power, territory, and resources arose as Thomas Hobbes argued in his bleak book, *Leviathan* (quoted above). The continued domination of the victor—often an empire, whether that of Alexander the Great, the Romans, British, or vis-à-vis super-power influence today—meant the peace it imposed was likely to survive any challenges, but for no longer than its power lasted.

Conclusion

The victor's peace framework has many flaws: it is subject to the problem of territorial and strategic over-extension and has limited ability to control 'unruly' subjects. In particular, hegemonic powers are often surprised by local resistance to their rule, as occupying powers, imperialists and colonials have all experienced in recent history. Such resistance is often aimed at broadening peace through self-determination, improving human rights and the distribution of economic resources. It may include resistance to totalitarianism as with much of the resistance to the control of the Soviet Union (the Prague Spring in 1968, the Polish resistance to their own government in the 1980s, or the collapse of the Berlin Wall in 1989). It may be non-violent, as with Indian resistance to the British Empire in the early 20th century during the independence campaign. However, often it leads to insurgencies, as with the attacks against US and other foreign targets in the 'statebuilding' mission in Afghanistan and Iraq in the 2000s. Indeed, power, however overwhelming in military, financial, political, or even normative terms, never quite seems to be enough to quell the local desire for autonomy, self-determination, and a positive form of peace. A lesson of history is that local consent and legitimacy are eventually needed for any victor's peace to be maintained and for it to advance into a more sophisticated form, if at all possible. A victor's peace may collapse if the hegemonic power loses interest in maintaining it or if resistance is widespread.

Chapter 4
Peace in history: towards the Enlightenment

War and violence are ever changing phenomena. There is a vast corpus of sources that make this clear: historical, social, religious, political and economic, artistic and cultural sources, as well as peace agreements, policies, theories, and philosophies. Early strands emerged in response to the limitations of the victor's peace, and were drawn together in more complex ways after the Enlightenment.

Peace treaties influenced the story of human history as much as wars or the succession of kings, queens, emperors, dictators, or elected leaders. They spanned examples such as the Kadesh Treaty (around 1274 BC) (see Figure 2) between the Hittite and Egyptian Empires to the more recent Comprehensive Peace Agreement signed between the two Sudanese sides in 2005. The framework of a peace treaty was used to end wars and stabilize regions: famous examples include the Pax Nicephori of AD 803 between the Roman Emperor Charlemagne and the Byzantine Empire; the Treaty of Venice of 1177 between the Catholic Pope, the north Italian city-states of the Lombard League, and Frederick I, the Holy Roman Emperor; or the Treaty of Perpetual Peace between England and Scotland in 1502 (see Figure 3). Perhaps most significant was the Treaty of Westphalia in 1648, which brought to an end a cycle of European wars. Other examples include the Paris Peace Treaty, which gave independence to the USA from Britain in

2. The Kadesh Treaty, from around 1274 BC, was one of the first ever recorded peace treaties between the Egyptian and Hittite Empires.

1783; the more famous Paris Peace Treaty at Versailles in 1919 after the First World War; and the UN Charter in 1945, which was essentially a peace treaty for the modern world. Other recent examples include the Camp David Agreement between Egypt and Israel in 1978 that brought to an end a cycle of wars between them; the Oslo Accords between Israel and the Palestinians in 1993; and the Dayton Agreement for Bosnia-Herzegovina in 1995, which through US pressure brought to an end the conflict between Serbs, Bosniacs, and Croats after three years of war.

Early strands: institutional and constitutional contributions

In ancient Mesopotamia, it was recognized that peace protects life, law, and customs, whereas war is aggressive and risks retaliation, as the Mosaic of Ur (c.2650 BC) portrays. Similarly,

3. The Treaty of Perpetual Peace signed by James IV of Scotland and Henry VII of England ended, for a time at least, 200 years of sporadic warfare between Scotland and England.

in the heroic Mesopotamian poem *Gilgamesh*, the hero's downfall is caused by his failure to preserve peace. The implication is clear. As in many of the world's religions, a historical propensity towards non-violence (though sometimes after a victory in war), Enlightenment, honesty, and integrity are generally presented as crucial to a peace that begins with the community and everyday life and then extends into the wider world.

The Cyrus Cylinder (6th century BC) is thought to be an early Persian declaration of human rights, illustrating an understanding of the breadth of the concept. Peace was also represented in early political philosophy such as in the thought of Confucius (551 BC–479 BC) on the connection between harmony at the individual level, in society, and at the international level. In classical literature such as Aristophanes' *Lysistrata* (*c.*411 BC), other dimensions were noted.

It was soon also apparent that peace processes and agreements were necessary to manage war and maintain order in the international system. In Plato's (428/427 BC–348/347 BC) *Republic*, Socrates argued that truth represents an ideal form associated with 'goodness' which sits uncomfortably with a race for power.

Understandings of religious tolerance were also commonly connected with peace, represented for example in Christianity by non-violence and pacifism. Similarly, there are the Buddhist and Hindi notions of *shanti* and *ahimsa*, which represent first an inner peace and then a wider peace. Islam and Sufi offer an understanding of peace as an internal quest within everyone, which when achieved may lead to an 'outer peace'. Hinduism, Buddhism, Christianity, Judaism, and Islam all make such claims in various different ways. Judaism associates peace with a sectarian identity within a universal peace. Christianity famously blessed its peacemakers in following suit. Islam demanded that any attempt at peacemaking should always be reciprocal and that individuals should be at peace before a wider peace can emerge. Most religions also warn of 'false peacemakers'. By the 10th century onward, a movement organized by the Catholic Church called the 'Peace of God' lobbied feudal elites and warlords to commit to peace rather than war. By the 11th century, a number of peace councils had been held in France, which the Pope supported, even though the Crusades were in full swing. In the last years of the 12th century, Richard the Lionheart commissioned his knights to keep order across his kingdom, calling them 'Justices of the Peace'. In the 13th century, the famous 'Prayer for Peace' appeared (attributed to Francis of Assisi): 'Lord, make me an instrument of Thy peace; where there is hatred, let me sow love...' Many religious orders began to emphasize peace.

Another early dimension of peace arose from pacts and leagues formed both to stabilize political relations and enable trade, such as the Hanseatic League of the 12th century. This was a commercial and defensive confederation of merchant guilds that controlled trade from the Baltic to the North Sea during the 13th–17th centuries. Others followed as European imperialism and colonialism gathered pace during the 16th and ensuing centuries, often between colonizers and local leaders, or between colonial powers that were seeking to demarcate their area of influence. Peace in these terms followed, and was secondary to, power and trade.

Perhaps one of the most famous early legal instruments of peace within a state was the English Magna Carta (1215). This bound even the king to the law (a radical idea in the 13th century), and introduced some basic aspects of human rights, including the principle of *Habeas Corpus* (meaning a citizen cannot be imprisoned without a fair trial) (see Figure 4).

Domestic peace was not the only preoccupation of government and law. Dante Alighieri, an early Florentine humanist, published an important book called *On World Government* in 1309, which

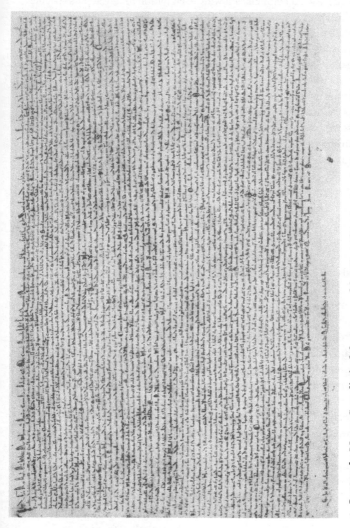

4. In 1215 the Magna Carta limited the powers of the King of England and protected his subjects' rights, forming the basis for the rule of law.

outlined how a world government and related justice system may resolve local conflicts, allowing each nation to develop its specific capacities in peacetime: '…[e]very kingdom divided against itself shall be laid waste…' To prevent this, '…there must therefore be one person who directs and rules mankind, and he is properly called "Monarch" or "Emperor". And thus it is apparent that the well-being of the world requires that there be a monarchy or empire' (Book 1). The idea of a world government, bound by law, became a long-standing motif of many peace movements. The state, government, and a concept of the 'international' now began to emerge as recognized components of a broader approach to peace.

There has also always been an 'art' of peace, such as in Renaissance painter Ambrogio Lorenzetti's *Allegory of Good and Bad Government* (1338–9) (see Figure 5). In two juxtaposed paintings he compared the beneficial and catastrophic effects of peace and war on a city, connecting peace not merely with the absence of war but the nature of political order.

Francisco de Vitoria (1483–1546), a Spanish Renaissance philosopher and jurist, explored the idea of the formation of a 'republic of the whole world'. He stated that the safety of diplomats should be assured, peace talks should be held to pre-empt conflict, and there should be a general acceptance of just terms. He also saw that it might be necessary to allow military intervention to prevent oppression. These terms should be the right of neutrality, safe passage, and restraint in the conduct of warfare (especially with regard to civilians).

By the 1500s, Erasmus had re-imagined a peace that rejected any order preserved by war, religion, or national identity. He was part of an emerging humanist tradition focused on how the internal structure of a state influenced its behaviour and how its Christian rulers should behave. His approach also called for binding

5. Lorenzetti's *Allegory of Good and Bad Government* (1338–9) depicts the benefits of good government on a city.

arbitration processes between states over their conflicts. In Erasmus' play *Complaint of Peace* (1517), a personified Peace said:

> ...am I not praised by both men and gods as the very source and defender of all good things? What is there of prosperity, of security, or of happiness that cannot be ascribed to me? On the other hand, is not war the destroyer of all things and the very seed of evil?

This play was published one year after Thomas More (1478–1535), another famous English Renaissance philosopher and humanist, published *Utopia* (1516), which explored the possibility of achieving a political and social utopia. The book had a notable cover, which depicted the contradictions of utopia. Erasmus' work also prepared the ground for Hugo Grotius (1583–1645), a Dutch jurist and philosopher, to develop international law.

International law was becoming an essential part of the international system and its approach to peace and the 'Treaty of Universal Peace' in 1520, negotiated by Cardinal Wolsey between England and France, offered hope that a wider European peace could for once be achieved. Erasmus went on to support, contra Machiavelli, welfare, representation, justice, laws, and education as essential to peace. He noted that '...[h]ardly any peace is so bad that it is not preferable to the most just war'.

There was a growing sense of how peaceful domestic and international order should be maintained. As representative political institutions in European states began to emerge, partly in response to social pressures and intellectual innovation, slowly replacing feudalism, parliaments began to emerge or re-form across Europe to assuage citizens who had begun to sense their capacity to lobby for, make, and preserve peace and social justice. Avoiding war, violence, conscription, and related tax burdens, as well as other indirect consequences of war, was becoming a political aim of increasingly demanding populations.

Peace was often formally 'made' by enlightened political and social leaders, emerging from diplomatic, elite, and high-level negotiations. It also balanced with interests according to 'red lines' delineated by imperial and state power. A painting of the Somerset House Conference in 1604 in London that brought to an end a 20-year war between England and Spain commemorates this approach.

Developments in peace thinking and practice were also taking place further afield. In Japan, a neo-Confucian scholar and shogun, Tokugawa Ieyasu, laid the basis for the Tokugawa Peace, which lasted from 1603 to 1868. This period saw significant economic growth as well as cultural development, but Japan was also isolationalist and had a strict social order. European settlers and explorers in the Americas also encountered indigenous communities that followed historical non-violent codes of behaviour (which the settlers themselves did not follow or accept, however).

Chapter 5
Peace in modernity:
the constitutional peace

Broader understandings of peace began to become more concrete with the emergence of stage two of the IPA after the First World War, drawing on intellectual work carried out from the 17th century onwards. The idea that peace could be constructed through law, institutions, rights, and prosperity, rather than by military power, emerged during and after the Enlightenment as an advance on the victor's peace. This was partly in response to violent excesses of elite power and partly to satisfy growing mobilization for a range of rights from within society.

Much of the discussion was carried out in the realms of a growing civil society and a network of social movements, intellectuals, and scientists, before being adopted by political elites and influencing the nature of the states-system. This order was to be founded upon the creation of both a domestic political and legal architecture and an international architecture designed to balance the interests, needs, and rights of the population. It would have the significant benefit of making the international order more sustainable because it would be based upon a positive peace. This would be achieved via a domestic constitutional peace, debated since Plato, Pericles, and Aristotle's discussions of the 'good life', and the merits of democracy versus the role of philosopher kings in ancient Greece. The theme of what shape good government should take was augmented by the Treaty of Westphalia in 1648, which connected the state to a peaceful and stable international order.

First steps

The flowering of peace thinking during the Enlightenment was intended to put an end to the lengthy and vicious cycle of elite-led or religious European wars (even if colonial wars further afield continued). Perhaps the most famous of the European peace treaties of this era was the Treaty of Westphalia. This was actually a series of peace treaties signed in 1648 in Osnabrück and Münster, which ended several connected wars (see Figure 6). These included the Thirty Years War (1618–48) of the Holy Roman Empire and the Eighty Years War (1568–1648) between Spain and the Dutch Republic. The treaty created a political order of sovereign states in Europe with the right of territorial integrity. It meant the state would not be subject to invasion or intervention

6. The swearing of the oath of ratification of the treaty of Münster in 1648, by Gerard Ter Borch, The Netherlands, 1648.

by other powers, a principle that still holds today (see UN Charter, Article 2/7). It was a precursor to future peace treaties, the development of international law and international organization, and the principle of self-determination.

The Enlightenment was partly the stimulus for an emerging idea that government, the state, and a system of international organizations should prioritize a general peace, rather than the vicarious interests of a few powerful actors in a Hobbesian 'state of nature' dominated by the Leviathan. Important contributions were made by Hugo Grotius and Emeric Cruce (1590–1648), the latter of whom published a book in 1623 subtitled 'Establishing a General Peace and Freedom of Trade', which castigated bigotry, glory, and profit-seeking through war. William Penn (1644–1718), a philosopher and founder of the Province of Pennsylvania, added his support for democracy and religious freedom. He began to develop 'internationalist' thinking, whereby international cooperation was deemed crucial for peace to emerge.

John Locke, an English philosopher regarded as one of the most influential of Enlightenment thinkers (1632–1704), offered the liberal idea that individualism, religious tolerance, and equality as well as consensual government were crucial for peace. Most important were law and civil society in his view:

> And that all men may be restrained from invading others rights, and from doing hurt to one another, and the law of nature be observed, which willeth the peace and preservation of all mankind, the execution of the law of nature is, in that state, put into every man's hands, whereby everyone has a right to punish the transgressors of that law to such a degree, as may hinder its violation…
>
> (*The Second Treatise of Civil Government*, 1690)

William Penn's essay 'Towards the Present and Future Peace of Europe' (1693) contributed to a discussion about how to organize a sustainable European peace through a parliament for Europe.

Rousseau (1712–78), a Genevan political philosopher who influenced the French Revolution, and Kant turned their attention to the refinement of a particular genre of European peace plan. Rousseau introduced the element of a contract between rulers and the people designed to balance the stability of the state with security as well as personal liberty, arguing: 'I prefer liberty with danger than peace with slavery.'

The constitutional peace

As the Enlightenment progressed the Hobbesian view that war was part of the natural fabric of international life, manipulated by Machiavellian princes, was replaced by the view that peace should be central to political life and institutions. Peace was achievable rather than merely an ideal to be aspired to—and this might be achieved by the concept of the nation-state and some form of international organization. Renaissance humanism (which developed during the 14th and 15th centuries AD) emphasized the need for a citizenry, including women, to engage in civic life in the state and follow virtuous courses of action. The liberalism that subsequently emerged challenged the idea that violence and war were part of the natural order of things. Peace could be the product of human ingenuity, especially if states and leaders could be sufficiently engaged with the latest thinking about the causes, types, and dynamics of violence. Enlightened actors with liberal views and objectives could now mitigate war, meaning that the behaviour of society and states could be moderated by new political systems and tools such as diplomacy and law, social movements, civil society, as well as external tools of intervention in crises.

Another important contribution was the historical argument that 'just war' should be waged by a legitimate authority only as a last resort and in response to an act of unjustified aggression. This had two effects: one, a growing concern with the nature of the type of state that would not be warlike, and two, an interest in international organization and institutions designed to prevent war.

The constant religious wars of that era in Europe were eventually brought to an end by an agreement along these lines, involving territorial states whose sovereignty might not be violated by other states. The implications were that territorial states and their international arrangements were necessary for a peace built either on common values or on an agreement to differ. Thus, the understanding of peace developed into a balance of power between states, guaranteed through international treaties and alliances, as was endorsed by the Treaty of Westphalia in 1648.

Clearly, this was not enough, and new thinking laid the constitutional foundations for stage two in the development of the architecture. Soon after Westphalia, John Locke argued that a law-based government would produce consensus, legitimacy, and therefore a domestic peace. A social contract was required in order to cement a consensual and representative relationship between leaders and society, the state providing security and acting as a 'neutral judge' to protect the lives, liberty, and property of citizens.

Free trade also emerged as an important component of the constitutional peace. Adam Smith's *Wealth of Nations* (1776) argued that international trade should be the basis of cooperation, prosperity, and peace between and within states.

The most substantial contribution came from Immanuel Kant, in his book *Perpetual Peace*. He based his subsequent understanding of peace upon the argument that even small-scale war or violence would escalate or echo around the world. He responded by suggesting the creation of just laws that would be reflected in a 'republican' or democratic political order. These conditions would crucially also prevent war between states. *Perpetual Peace* laid out the conditions through which an early form of social justice could be attained within states and peace could be achieved between states (later to be reflected in the UN Charter in 1945).

Kant's view was much more complicated than the geopolitical balancing system of stage one, however, which effectively mitigated power relations in the 19th century, but did little to resolve them. Kant argued that:

> The universal and lasting establishment of peace constitutes not merely a part, but the whole final purpose and end of the science of right as viewed within the limits of reason.

Kant's point-by-point articulation of a peaceful world order was as follows:

> (1) No conclusion of Peace shall be held to be valid as such, when it has been made with the secret reservation of the material for a future War.
>
> (2) No State having an existence by itself—whether it be small or large—shall be acquirable by another State through inheritance, exchange, purchase or donation.
>
> (3) Standing Armies shall be entirely abolished in the course of time.
>
> (4) No National Debts shall be contracted in connection with the external affairs of the State.
>
> (5) No State shall intermeddle by force with the Constitution or Government of another State.
>
> (6) No State at war with another shall adopt such modes of hostility as would necessarily render mutual confidence impossible in a future Peace...

He added the requirements that:

> The Civil Constitution in every State shall be Republican [meaning democratic].

The Right of Nations shall be founded on a Federation of Free States.

The Rights of men as Citizens of the world in a cosmo-political system, shall be restricted to conditions of universal Hospitality.

He called for the creation of an international organization to promote world peace, and for states to adopt democracy and human rights (which eventually emerged after the First World War). This was crucial to the peace movements of the 20th century and since. It foreshadowed the establishment of international organization after the Second World War and a range of institutions, from the UN system to the EU and the African Union, as well as the contemporary mechanisms of peacemaking, peacebuilding, statebuilding, and humanitarian intervention. It became the basis for the democratic or liberal peace after the end of the Cold War. Kant wrote:

> [I]f the consent of the citizens is required in order to decide that war should be declared (and in this constitution it cannot but be the case), nothing is more natural than that they would be very cautious in commencing such a poor game, decreeing for themselves all the calamities of war. Among the latter would be: having to fight, having to pay the costs of war from their own resources, having painfully to repair the devastation war leaves behind, and, to fill up the measure of evils, load themselves with a heavy national debt that would embitter peace itself and that can never be liquidated on account of constant wars in the future.

Following these constitutional strands of thinking about peace and order, Jeremy Bentham (1748–1832), a British philosopher and social reformer, added a concern with a number of social issues: welfare, economic freedom, the separation of church and state, freedom of expression, equal rights for women, and the abolition of slavery and the death penalty. He offered the utilitarian insight for government that the greatest happiness for the greatest good would lead to peace, as the British economist

David Ricardo (1772–1823) confirmed in an economic sense. Despite the criticism from British economist Thomas Malthus (1766–1834), who believed that surplus populations would lead to unsustainable development, resource depletion, and war, the free trade argument continued to be an essential pillar of the emerging version of peace. However, it was propagated through an uncomfortable mixture of British liberalism and colonialism until the 20th century.

Liberal thinking was beginning to crystallize into more than speculation: John Stuart Mill (1806–73), a British philosopher, connected development with peace, individual liberty, and private property. He claimed that peace lay in both the protection of individual freedoms and the existence of effective government, essentially forming a constitutional peace framework that would create a positive social contract between citizen and state and, through international cooperation and trade, pacify geopolitics.

In the 20th century the democratic peace argument came to be regarded as one of the only 'laws' of international relations. After the end of the Cold War it has been defined by democracy, free trade, and human rights, as Francis Fukuyama notably described in his essay 'The End of History and the Last Man' (1989), which celebrated the potential for the spread of democracy after the end of the Cold War. This became firmly embedded in the overall international architecture of peace, in many states' constitutions, international law, the role of donors, the UN, International Nongovernmental Organizations (INGOs), and International Financial Institutions (IFIs) like the World Bank. As a result, many of the world's states that have emerged from imperial war, world war, wars of decolonization, and from the collapse of communism have liberal-democratic institutions and constitutions (63 per cent according to Freedom House in 2013 at its peak, but declining ever since then), which also involve a commitment to human rights. It is notable that the European Union today owes a great deal of its constitutional structure to the

Enlightenment peace projects, which promoted the constitutional peace.

Several states went even further during the last century in their pursuit of peace: according to German Basic Law, Germany is not allowed to have offensive armed forces (a relic of Allied occupation after the Second World War); Japan (at least until recently) is said likewise to have a 'peace constitution', and other countries like Costa Rica have completely dismantled their armed forces.

Limitations

The problem with Kant's assumption that states act to maximize the interests of their own peoples (where they treat them as means rather than ends) is that states and elites may be predatory actors instead. The line between contributing to peace and following a nationalist or elite interest was, and is, finely drawn. The emergence of nationalism was also a consequence of what John Stuart Mill identified as the right of people to determine their own government. This may mean pursuing a national interest and identity not necessarily commensurate with regional or international peace or universal norms. As the principle of national self-determination gained popular appeal in the last 100 or so years, especially during the dissolution of the Ottoman and Austro-Hungarian, French, British, and other European empires after the First and Second World Wars, and at the end of the Cold War (e.g. in the Balkans), the concepts of both nationalism and ethno-nationalism became associated with the foundations not of order but of war. This soon became a spark for war between groups laying claim to the same territory. It continues to do so in the contemporary era, as in the cases of Cyprus, Sudan, Bosnia-Herzegovina, Israel/Palestine, and others.

Another concern has been that the constitutional peace has been characterized as a Eurocentric enterprise, and its secular nature was problematic for many. Nevertheless, the democratic or liberal peace argument does seem to have held. One of the most significant exceptions has been that democracies may still fight wars against non-democracies, for a range of reasons, as the cases of military intervention in Afghanistan and Iraq in the early 2000s illustrated. The democratic peace framework also assumes conflict-affected states will evolve into democracies. This has often not been the case, however, and many peace processes are hindered by wars or authoritarianism, as with Cambodia or in the Israel–Palestine conflict. In addition, the constitutional peace focused on an elite-level official discourse by state and government, and is geographically and temporally bounded by territorial sovereignty. It continues to be underpinned by the victor's peace and the use of force.

As a further caveat, Kant once remarked that *perpetual peace* might turn out to be rather unpleasant. Incessant materialism and the related consumption of raw materials might ultimately lead to a hollow victory and even to environmental collapse. In practice the application of the constitutional peace has often been blocked by actors who do not want to share power and who oppose domestic legal structures that might outlaw their authoritarian or corrupt activities. This has not changed since Hitler and Mussolini ignored the League of Nations in the 1920s and 1930s, or when Saddam Hussein ignored the UN over his invasion of Kuwait in the 1990s and blocked inspections of his possible weapons of mass destruction programme in the early 2000s.

Chapter 6
The next step: an institutional peace

The 19th-century English poet Alfred, Lord Tennyson (1809–92) lauded the potential of international cooperation and law (as well as making an implicit reference to democracy) in his poem 'Locksley Hall' (1837–8):

> Till the war-drum throbb'd no longer, and the battle-flags were furl'd,
> In the Parliament of man, the Federation of the World.

He pointed to an institutional form of peace, which has been very significant in the modern era, and also fundamental to stage two in the development of the IPA. The role of international institutions and law in supporting the consolidation of a constitutional peace within and between states represented the next step in building a positive peace. The institutional peace began to develop around the same time as the constitutional peace became prominent, during the Enlightenment. By the second half of the 20th century the UN, international donors, international law, and a range of regional actors, notably the EU and the African Union, coalesced around a more dynamic approach with the aim of creating a wide-ranging positive peace.

The institutional peace aims to anchor states within a specific set of values and a shared legal context through which they agree multilaterally how to behave. They also agree to police and enforce that behaviour on the part of 'renegade' states. Before the era of states, kings and queens tried to achieve this through alliances, peace treaties, marriages, trusteeships, and other forms of political relationship. Alexander the Great (356–323 BC) used many of these techniques to hold together his expanding empire. Two millennia later, the leaders of the emerging states in Europe began to institutionalize recurrent high-level diplomatic conferences. These were often held to debate matters of war and peace and so were perceived as a way out of the cycles of violence that the victor's peace had given rise to.

An emerging set of intentional institutions were created to cement a stable international order, complementary to the growing belief that liberal democratic states were less likely to go to war with each other. If states share common goals of peace and free trade, they may organize themselves into an international community (and may even submit themselves to world government or a world federation, as many early 20th-century idealists hoped, including writers such as H. G. Wells (1866–1946)). The IPA was becoming more substantial, enabling states and empires to balance their interests and find agreement about, and follow, international norms and international law.

The early development of international institutions

The institutional peace is part of a cosmopolitan ethic dating back to Diogenes the Cynic (c.412–323 BC), who declared himself a cosmopolitan. This idea posited that despite people's many differences a universally shared morality as well as international cooperation was possible, and that a world government might eventually be desirable. It found its contemporary character in the peace project associated with the Enlightenment. The Grotian discourse on natural law also made an important contribution, dictating coexistence and non-intervention between states. States have a right of self-defence following 'just war' thinking.

The formation of institutions intended to prevent war gathered pace almost simultaneously. Much of its progress followed the ideas of 17th-century philosophers such as the Duc de Sully's (1560–1641) work on a 'grand design'. This was a plan to stop religious war, start an international organization consisting of European powers, operate a balance of power mechanism via a permanent assembly of ambassadors, and dissolve the European empires. The plan influenced Kant's work, illustrating how international institutions could solve the dangerous instability of the stage one balance of power mechanism, as was soon apparent after 1815. Diplomacy, international institutions, law, connected to public opposition to violence were crucial.

The Abbé de Saint-Pierre (1658–1743), an influential French writer, proposed in his book *Project for Perpetual Peace* (1713) an international organization responsible for maintaining peace. This was the start of a formal Enlightenment genre of peace projects, spurring Kant and others to develop these ideas further in the face of continuing European wars. Saint-Pierre's peace plan was essentially a European treaty for a federation of states, in which law would be founded upon justice, equality, and reciprocity. Saint-Pierre called for the Christian (and also Muslim) sovereigns of Europe to form a permanent union for peace and security. This organization would not intervene in the affairs of member states but would have intelligence and self-defence capacities and might even send in troops to preserve peace.

William Penn also wanted to see a form of European parliament, in order to achieve 'peace with justice', and Kant insisted that the rule of law envisaged by the democratic, constitutional peace he had argued for should be extended to international relations.

This fell short of the establishment of a world government, but instead suggested a multilateral system of states:

> Reason would drive [states] to give up their savage lawless freedom, to accommodate themselves to public coercive laws, and thus to form an ever-growing State of Nations, such as would at last embrace all the Nations of the Earth. But as the Nations, according to their ideas of international Right, will not have such a positive rational system, and consequently reject in fact what is right in theory, it cannot be realised in this pure form. Hence, instead of the positive idea of a Universal Republic—if all is not to be lost—we shall have as result only the negative surrogate of a Federation of the States averting war, subsisting in an external union, and always extending itself over the world.
>
> (Kant, *Perpetual Peace*)

A controversial issue was and is whether this takes the form of a multilateral system of states or a world government. Kant feared that a world government would be as unpleasant as a Hobbesian world as it might culminate in worse despotism through the concentration of powers in one central government. Thus, *Perpetual Peace* eventually found itself reflected in the UN Charter, but as Kant specified, international order rests at best on a federation of free states. Furthermore, he argued, these should abolish war and offer non-citizens 'universal hospitality'. International trade would also be beneficial.

Several steps occurred in the development of the institutional peace framework. The Treaty of Westphalia (1648) created an unstable states system as a response to Europe's religious wars, but also provided an impetus for international organizations to develop in order to maintain peace between states. The Congress of Vienna in 1815 saw a system of international institutions begin to become a reality to deal with the states system's inconsistencies, as seen in the Napoleonic Wars and the race for European domination that caused them. The Congress of Vienna represented the attempt of statesmen such as Metternich, Castlereagh, and Talleyrand to create a realist balance of power which, however, depended upon their capacity for diplomacy and to intervene in the affairs of other states. It was primarily an instrument of British 'order creation' and thus was very close to also being a victor's peace despite its institutionalization upon the European stage.

These developments were indicative of a growing rejection of the idea that war was endemic and inevitable. The conservatives and liberals of this era saw peace and war in different ways. The conservatives believed that peace lay in the preservation of the existing order, perhaps through the use of war, and certainly through a class system and gender and racial hierarchies. Liberals believed that peace would be achieved through a transformation brought about by economic and social progress, for which war (and possibly the state) was an unwanted obstacle. Nationalists formed a third grouping, believing that nations had a right to self-determination and potentially to dominate other states, through the use of force if necessary.

Peace in 19th-century Europe was disrupted by the growing forces of nationalism and by the constant imperial and colonial conflicts fought in North America, Asia, and Africa in search of an empire. Wars glorified nationalism, preserved the wealth of the old conservative order, and were part of a civilizing mission for liberals. Industrialization was also making the scale of war greater and far more deadly than ever before.

Disparate reforms and dynamics assisted the emergence of the institutional peace. Disarmament and rights campaigns were often largely run from within civil society, but often became internationalized through rudimentary networks, sometimes also connected to state-run humanitarian campaigns. These began to coalesce. For example, from 1816 to the 1860s Britain deployed a naval squadron against slave trading on the west coast of Africa. This reversal in the British approach to slavery meant a reinterpretation of international law to allow vessels to be boarded and searched. For the first time, perhaps, a humanitarian principle took precedence over the interests of the powerful, which would henceforth be crucial for the emerging set of international institutions.

Another dimension was provided by Henri Dunant's work leading to the Geneva Convention of 1864, and the creation of the International Committee of the Red Cross (ICRC) gave rise to what is now known as international humanitarian law. The ICRC is the oldest humanitarian organization, and is charged with the mandate (through international treaty) of being the custodian of the laws of war.

By the turn of the century, the idea of liberal internationalism appeared to be gathering pace. Major peace conferences were held at The Hague in 1899 and 1907, which also led to the eventual establishment of the Permanent International Court of Justice in 1922. In 1910 a Universal Peace Congress examined the need for international law, self-determination, and an end to colonialism. In 1913, another disarmament congress followed to mark the opening of the Peace Palace in The Hague, funded by the American industrialist Andrew Carnegie. Yet, in reality, during the early 20th century, it was also readily apparent that Europe and the world were sliding towards a major war and the existing tools for peacemaking were too limited to prevent it.

The institutional peace after the First World War

The institutional peace framework gained its most sophisticated apparatus after the world wars of the 20th century. US President Wilson's 'Fourteen Points' presented at the Versailles peace talks after the First World War were foundational in the emergence of a modern notion of peace with both institutional and constitutional dimensions. He called for the foundation of the League of Nations to guarantee the sovereignty and territorial integrity of all states. The League was to be an international mechanism of conflict management that should prevent war for the successor states of many of the now collapsing empires.

The post-First World War settlement was guided by the principle that territorial adjustments should be of benefit to the populations concerned—in other words, self-determination. Wilson believed that this represented a peace without victory: yet it also represented a unilateral American pronouncement. The Versailles Treaty accentuated democratization within a state framework and regulated interstate relations, thus combining a constitutional and institutional framework for peace. President Wilson had in mind an 'ultimate peace of the world' reminiscent of Kant's perpetual peace. It was to rest on a 'community of power' and represented an 'organised common peace' to lay to rest the failures of imperialism, geopolitics, and fix the balance of power system of stage one of the IPA. It was to be a 'peace without victory, a peace among equals'. Wilson told the US Congress early in April 1917 that the 'world must be made safe for democracy'. Perhaps most importantly a form of social justice was now being seen as essential to a universal peace and rights were becoming more prominent.

As it transpired Versailles was regarded as a victor's peace, and this was its fatal flaw. This was exactly the fear underlying Keynes's famous critique, specifically of the War Guilt Clause (Article 231), which blamed Germany for aggression, and of the level of reparations to be paid by Germany. The way in which the Allies had established agreements while applying blame and financial responsibility to Germany and its allies meant that there would not be a stable peace resulting from the treaty. German democracy would be 'annihilated' in the very process of trying to construct it. Some commentators, like E. H. Carr (1892–1982), who was a British delegate at the Versailles conference, believed the emerging institutional peace to be utopian and implausible.

There were also other competing versions of dynamics in the post-war order. One was based upon the notion of a historical dialectic of progress and a classless society, supported by the Soviet Union. Others derived from imperialism and nationalism and the decolonization of empire. The major obstacle to Wilson's new layer of the IPA was that no state was prepared to take responsibility or provide guarantees for it. The US Congress did not want to be responsible at this level; Britain, France, and Germany still harboured their antipathies to each other; some statesmen and politicians still sought to justify imperialism and colonialism; Soviet Russia was concerned with its own revolution; militant nationalism was on the rise in Japan and elsewhere; and the collapse of the Ottoman and Austro-Hungarian Empires had left significant spoils to be fought over. The peace architecture that had been created at Versailles was deeply flawed in practice, and was made even more fragile by the financial crises of the late 1920s, which created socio-economic difficulties at a time when radical ideologies were making themselves widely felt.

Chapter 7
A radical phase: a civil peace and social advocacy

The discussion of peace had by the 19th century ceased to be dominated by kings, philosophers, religious figures, or political theorists. With the birth of an array of social movements, activists, and advocates for peace, involving ordinary people who were determined to wrest the power to make war away from elites, it became clear that peace partly lay in their hands too. Yet, at this point such actors were not included in what was essentially a geopolitically organized peace architecture.

The importance of social advocacy

It is important to note the significance of the American Revolution, which from 1774 rejected European aristocratic forms of leadership, in favour of republicanism and liberalism. Social mobilization for peace stimulated liberal political declarations such as the US Declaration of Independence (1776), where the rights of men were laid out succinctly (life, liberty, and the pursuit of happiness) (see Figure 7). Similarly, the French Revolutions from 1789 saw the monarchy replaced by popular mobilization for similar principles of equality, citizenship, democracy, secularism, and basic human rights. These Western revolutions sought to devolve power to the population away from the lineage of royalty or colonialism, to attain personal freedom and representative government. Consequently, in the light of the realization of the

7. **The Declaration of Independence also brought to an end the war between the 13 American colonies and Great Britain in 1776.**

potential of the political role of the individual and the possibilities of mass mobilization, often in non-violent ways, non-state actors began to gain a significant political role. This was by campaigning for more rights, against multiple forms of discrimination, and for humanitarian assistance.

Momentum grew in the 19th century through the creation of the ICRC, the mobilization of various social justice-oriented movements, the abolition of the slave trade by the English Parliament in 1807, the campaigns for and introduction of voting rights, the development of international law, and the growing popularity of disarmament campaigns. Many other activities organized by non-state actors were aimed at political, social, and economic reform.

Historically, a mixture of social movements have contributed to pressure for a significant change in politics and social structures, often in response to long-standing political, social, and economic inequalities across and between societies. This indicated that peace required changes to the nature of political authority, the state, and the international order itself. Such movements followed on from the success of the civil society movements against slavery in the 19th century and began to organize and mobilize across a range of other issue areas, most notably for disarmament by the end of the century. In Britain, the Chartists, an amalgam of working-class organizations which desired political reform in Britain between 1838 and 1848, published their agenda for universal suffrage (for men at least), regular elections, and a professional political cohort (as opposed to a landed aristocracy). There was a socialist tinge to such developments along the path to social justice, whereby society and individuals pressed for equality rather than hierarchy, and from the perspective of the 'proletariat' aimed to resist exploitation and create a classless society.

Karl Marx's (1818–83) work was instrumental in the development of the socialist movement and its internationalization. He outlined the problems of industrialization and capitalism from the perspective of the 'working classes'. In his book with another revolutionary socialist, Friedrich Engels, *The Communist Manifesto* (published in 1848), Marx criticized the structural oppression that capitalism and the old feudal system represented, supporting the provision of better conditions and rights for workers. He was, however, ambivalent about whether peaceful or revolutionary means were necessary. Such sentiments also reflected a broader social dissatisfaction with the hierarchical organization of power and class in the industrializing West, with implications for both war and peace, imperialism, capitalism, and the state. His thought was also influential for many societies after waves of decolonization in the 1950s and 1960s. Many social movements challenged existing closed political orders (often seen as a communitarian form of politics), imperialism, inequality, and discrimination, and advocated for shared norms and coexistence (cosmopolitanism, or later 'pluriversalism'). Social advocacy opened up social justice issues, which also would ultimately connect global justice with peace.

A major international peace conference in Britain in 1843 saw support for free trade, pacifism, and peaceful means of conflict resolution begin to coalesce. Another conference was held in Paris the following year. Richard Cobden (1804–65), one of the great English liberal thinkers of the day, and Victor Hugo (1802–85), the French poet and novelist, were in attendance, illustrating the breadth of the appeal of such ambitions. At this meeting, the pace and pressures of development, the shrinking of the world due to better transport and communication, the need for mediation systems between great powers, and the dangerous habit of raising loans for wars were all discussed. There was disagreement, however, over the mutually exclusive agendas of disarmament, pacifism, the maintenance of security, and self-determination, which divided participants (and continue to do so). However, concerted international attention was turning to the creation and consolidation of mechanisms, devices, and tools to deal with different elements of war, as well as to maintain order and make peace. This included international law and institutions, mediation and diplomacy, disarmament, the nature of the political economy of the international and states system, and social mobilization. These efforts were developing across politics, security, law, and economic issues areas, also incorporating social and artistic endeavours.

Organizations like the Fabian Society, founded in England in 1884, worked at improving social and working conditions and tempered any revolutionary intent with a Christian ethos. Even so, it was the implications of such thinking about social justice, spanning human rights and representation to a fairer distribution of power and resources across society, as well as disarmament, that produced one of the most powerful reformist dynamics of the 19th and 20th centuries. As such thinking developed, however, it began to raise concerns about the nature of the international system, and in particular (after the attempts to end slavery in the 19th century) the links between capitalism and colonial, imperial, and racial frameworks of politics. Peacemaking had ramifications for the nature of the state and the international system itself, and in the 19th century both were increasingly seen as anachronistic in ethical terms.

One solution to these endemic problems was non-violence. Pacifist movements were sometimes related also to various long-standing peace churches, notably the Quaker and Mennonite movements, dating back to the 16th century. They have made an important contribution, as have public debates about non-violent resistance, the actions of conscientious objectors, civil disobedience, and various forms of anarchism. Pacifism is often equated with peace movements (though not all are pacifist because some argue that there are occasions—such as for self-defence, to resist oppression, genocide, or imperialism—where violence may be justified). In general pacifists oppose war and violence of all sorts. Pacifism has been a feature of human history and all of the different world religions. Tolstoy's and Thoreau's writings on the need for pacifism and on civil disobedience become especially significant during this period. Leo Tolstoy (1828–1910) was the Russian author of *War and Peace*, and a noted moral thinker and social reformer, often described as a 'Christian anarchist' and pacifist. Tolstoy became famous for opposing militarism through civil disobedience and non-violent resistance. Henry David Thoreau (1817–62), an American philosopher, also published an important essay, 'Civil Disobedience', in which he called upon individuals to resist unjust states:

> If a thousand men were not to pay their tax bills this year, that would not be a violent and bloody measure, as it would be to pay them, and enable the State to commit violence and shed innocent blood. This is, in fact, the definition of a peaceable revolution, if any such is possible.

Increasingly, non-violent resistance aimed to overcome inequality and injustice and was deployed by large social interest groups. Ideas on non-violent resistance were to have a profound impact on Mahatma Gandhi (1869–1948) during the Indian independence struggle from the British Empire in the first half of the 20th century, and also on Martin Luther King, Jr (1929–68), during his civil rights struggle in the USA.

Another aspect of peace thought emerged from the work of one of the key early thinkers in the anarchist tradition, Pierre-Joseph Proudhon. He argued in his study *War and Peace* (1861) that nation-states and the principle of private property would undermine peace. He thought that anarchism should be non-violent and systems of mutualism (whereby labour would receive a fair recompense rather than make profit for capitalists) should take over the formal processes of the state.

Similar themes were on the agenda of the First and Second Internationals (1864–76 and 1889–1916) towards the end of the 19th century, which brought together a range of socialist and labour parties from around 20 different countries, to promote the rights of workers. Working men's associations, trade unions, socialists, and communists around the world, but most notably in Britain, tried (often unsuccessfully) to develop a united front on matters such as working rights and hours, gender equality, and a limited anti-war stance. Peace was beginning to be connected with the development of capitalism and its modes of production and was being contested on ideological grounds.

By the end of the 19th century, the emerging peace movements had involved or gained the attention of millions of people.

They increasingly refused to be passive actors in elite-led imperial or colonial wars and began to develop a range of political, philosophical, economic, and social arguments and tools against war, to be used for a better framework of peace. Various 'friends of peace' movements in the West laid the basis for an organized peace movement to emerge. In Britain and the USA, they united a range of thinkers, religious movements, labourers, scientists, writers, economists, social reformers, and activists. Their aim was to prevent rulers from seeing only benefit in war, but also to realize the potential of peace as well as popular demand for it. The Quakers, for example, equated pacifism and peace with religious positions connected to a broader struggle for justice and welfare (and today they quietly support civil society and formal peace processes throughout the world).

The increasingly industrial-scale conflicts of the 19th century, from the Crimean War to various Franco-Prussian wars from the 1850s to the 1870s, led to the emergence of another important strand of peace architecture. This lay in the beginnings of humanitarian law and of humanitarian relief organizations, notably the Red Cross. In 1859 Henri Dunant, a Swiss businessman, was an incidental witness of war. Horrified by his experience of the Battle of Solferino, he inspired the establishment of the International Red Cross in Geneva in 1863. The subsequent first Geneva Convention called for the humane treatment of all involved in war, including prisoners and humanitarian workers. It required that the Red Cross, a neutral international humanitarian relief agency, should have free access to war zones and its neutrality be respected by warring governments. Dunant was to be a joint recipient of the first Nobel Peace Prize in 1901.

The various 19th-century peace movements culminated in a number of congresses, movements, meetings, and conferences, including the 1899 and 1907 conferences at The Hague, which led to the Hague Conventions. These produced the first formal statements on war crimes and disarmament. They became connected to what was becoming known as 'liberal internationalism', which developed the goal of formalizing the peace movement at the international level. One strand of this development sought to refine international law, another focused on creating an international federation of states, whilst another looked towards a world government, as the ultimate arbiter of peace. The 1899 conference introduced the idea of international arbitration as a means of dispute settlement (in which conflict parties agree to submit their disputes to binding resolution by a third party). This was supposed to be obligatory upon all of its state signatories, 26 of whom were present. No progress was made on the issue of disarmament, however. Further conferences were held in the early part of the 20th century, which also included women's peace movements, but the outbreak of the First World War put such developments in abeyance until the League of Nations was formed by the victorious Allies soon after.

The arts also played their role in the dissemination of the concept of peace, and its popularization. For example, Lorenzetti's 1340 frescos of *Peace and War* in Siena illustrated the radically different impacts of peace and war on the city. Sometimes, peace was inferred in subtle and unlikely forms, such as Rubens's famous painting *Minerva protects Pax from Mars* (1629–30), which was an illustration of the painter's role as unofficial envoy between England and Spain. During the 20th century peace continued to motivate or be reflected in numerous examples of modern art and culture, such as Picasso's *Guernica* (1937), which exposed the effects of modern industrial warfare against civilians, and in literature and war poetry, such as that of Wilfred Owen, British poet and a soldier in the First World War (including 'Dulce et Decorum Est' and 'Anthem for Doomed Youth', 1919).

Historically, from the perspective of civil society, a period of violence in any society or at international level has always spurred the development of peacemaking strategies to combat it, both from within society and by external actors. Many so-called 'peaceful societies' around the world, often of a small, tribal nature, developed small-scale internal processes of conflict mediation, avoidance, and self-restraint. The state and international peace architecture have reflected this on a larger scale. In modern times, some states have adopted 'peace constitutions', whereby they have little or no military capacity. Some states see themselves as pacific, such as Costa Rica, Japan, and Germany, according to their post-Second World War constitutions.

Social and advocacy movements were supported by new technologies of communication, transport, and trade. Two distinct early pathways can be observed, including secular or religious orientations. They may have been derived from the secular emergence of liberal internationalism, associated with campaigns against conscription, ideological and feminist movements against war and for conventional disarmament, the Campaign for Nuclear Disarmament (CND), and environmental movements. Many later resistance movements have also described themselves as peace movements, whether they were resisting authoritarian or colonial rule or working towards modernization, development, human rights, and democracy.

As international humanitarian law gradually influenced the state's understanding of war, it reinforced a more inclusive discourse of peace within the international system. By the 20th century, individuals had begun to lobby elites, leaders, and officials for peace in an organized manner. Partly because of such mobilization, The Hague peace conferences of 1899 and 1907, the International Court of Justice, and the 1910 and 1913 Universal Peace Congresses all pointed to the need for international law, self-determination, and an end to colonialism. Non-state actors were directly involved with the International Labour Organization from its establishment, and though they were excluded from The Hague Conferences in 1899 and 1907, their very exclusion was also an acknowledgement of their significance. Later, the League of Nations also provided non-state actors with informal consultative status.

Such organizations soon began to proliferate: the International Rescue Committee (IRC) began its life rescuing Jews from Europe during the Second World War, and was later to be involved with retrieving Hungarian refugees after the failure of the 1956 uprising and Cuban refugees after Fidel Castro came to power in Cuba in 1959. Other such organizations followed, including the Catholic Relief Service, World Vision, and the Oxford Committee for Famine Relief (OXFAM).

Such efforts put positive forms of peace at the forefront of international and academic thinking. There was a growing recognition of the requirement of social justice for individuals and communities, and not just treaties or disarmament for or between states if peace and order was to be both just and sustainable.

This view of a positive peace for civil society had an impact on the international system too. The Non-Aligned Movement, for example, wanted to propose an alternative approach to politics and development during the Cold War. This view was quietly influential, and the movement now includes nearly two-thirds of the UN's member states. Along with the debates of the era that connected self-determination, equality, and human rights to the growing relationship between peace and order, this development also extended the idea of rights to relate to the needs of decolonized societies, which had rapidly increased in number (outnumbering the West in the UN General Assembly by the late 1960s).

Social peace movements, ensuing constitutional frameworks, and related international strategies to prevent war did constrain the forces of war and power at state and international levels. They built local to international networks across formal and informal groupings and actors. They focused on specific issues, such as disarmament, non-violence, equality, self-determination, or a peace process for a specific regional war elsewhere in the world. By the 20th century these movements had contributed to the IPA, setting the stage for the transnational, transversal social movements of the second half of the 20th century, which focused on decolonization, self-determination, human rights, development, and equality.

The civil peace

The development of social movements and advocacy focused on peace opened up a further strand of the evolution of peace: the civil peace. According to this approach, every individual in society has the capacity to mobilize for peace from a variety of different perspectives, whether for disarmament, for international cooperation, or against violence, discrimination, and oppression. It relates to the historical phenomena of social direct action for political, economic, and identity reasons, of citizen advocacy and mobilization, in the attainment or defence of basic human rights and values. It is also related to pacifism in its main forms, where civil action is non-violent in principle. Without the civil peace and its social forms of mobilization, international and constitutional frameworks would not be legitimated by ordinary people.

Indeed, it is plausible to argue that many elements of the IPA emerged first within civil society, according to intellectual, ethical, social, economic, and political responses to war and violence at state and international levels. Philosophers and thinkers, scientists, advocates, and activists throughout history have often provided the script for the reform of politics after war. This is when a synergy between advanced thought and powerful actors seems most likely to emerge. This synergy gave rise the Congress of Vienna, the League of Nations, the UN, and the EU, amongst others. It was obscure 17th-century thought from within civil society that gave rise to the 20th century's liberal international and domestic peace settlements.

The civil peace often arises from localized organizations and their campaigns, which are normally connected transnationally to other similar movements around the world. These networks traverse the lines between formal and informal politics, grass roots, state, and international actors. They are connected to ethics, knowledge, and science, and expand rapidly over time. Civil society develops as local organizations, communities, and political actors coalesce around the various dynamics and requirements of peace with justice, as the causes of violence are identified by those on the receiving end. It has often represented a challenge to structural and direct violence embedded in the hierarchies of the states system or within society itself (i.e. a negative peace).

The growing role of NGOs

An important development for the evolution of the IPA and its growing incorporation of non-state actors related to the proliferation of non-governmental organizations. Their expertise, ethics, and determination played an important role in highlighting the need for human rights to be included in the UN Charter at San Francisco in 1945, and helped draft the Universal Declaration of Human Rights. They were significant in advocating for, and drafting, different UN treaties and conventions spanning issues from the elimination of discrimination against women (1979) to the rights of children (1989). They played important roles in many other human rights-related UN working groups, as well as in the creation of the position of the UN High Commissioner for Human Rights. They consolidated the relationship between social movements and civil society and the design, often from the top down, of a more pacific state and international system. They promoted the expansion of rights in conflict-affected societies as well as in domestic and international law, treaties, and doctrine. They also acted as a bridge into stage four of the IPA, and the liberal peace framework later in the century.

Humanitarian law provides the legal context in which NGOs operate. One of the key early examples of contemporary humanitarianism was the Biafra crisis of 1968, when the Igbo people attempted to secede from Nigeria, causing the Nigerian

Civil War. Despite their challenge to the sovereignty of Nigeria during this crisis, humanitarian aid NGOs mobilized regardless of international disapproval. This was repeated several times during the 1970s, in various crises in Bangladesh, Ethiopia, and Cambodia. Civil societies and NGOs were beginning to mobilize around the world to advocate for human rights, democracy, and emergency humanitarian assistance for the victims of war.

From these strands emerged a powerful body of actors and a language of rights, development, and norms that reinforced the view that individuals had legitimate rights for security, basic needs, autonomy, and to their own identity.

There are now so many NGOs around the world it is almost impossible to count them, especially those local NGOs working in post-conflict and development contexts. The most familiar international NGOs working on peacebuilding and human rights include International Crisis Group, International Alert, Amnesty International, and Human Rights Watch. Amnesty International, for example, was founded in 1961, part of the huge international human rights movement that was emerging. The Helsinki Final Act spurred the growth of civil society movements, NGOs, and the support of human rights in 1975.

Many more NGOs formed in the 1990s as a response to the broad requirements of the synthesis of peacebuilding, humanitarianism, human rights monitoring, and advocacy. They were to support a burgeoning civil society in post-conflict zones, which would then form the basis for a social contract and the liberal peace. It was partly because of civil society activism for human rights that the concept of humanitarian intervention emerged.

Organizations like ICRC, Médecins Sans Frontières (MSF), and the International Crisis Group (ICG), among many others, have also played an important role in other aspects of civil society, development, and assistance. NGOs are now a recognized part of the UN system, hold consultative status within the United Nations' platform on economic and social issues ECOSOC, and are an integral part of the humanitarian discourse. Under Article 71 of the UN Charter, ECOSOC is empowered to consult with NGOs on economic and social issues, as well as on matters relating to refugees, the environment, and development. This is particularly important in the context of debates about human security and the emergence of a 'global civil society' in stage four of the IPA. It rests upon a global network of local NGOs with informal and formal connections, and often a common agreement on the underlying norms, rights, and processes of peace and development. This has increasingly supported peace, development, and security where states have failed.

However, there have been problems with such development. Civil society has become overloaded. Donor and humanitarian assistance may have contradictory effects. UNRWA (the United Nations Relief and Works Agency for Palestine Refugees), created in 1949 to provide relief and development for more than 5 million Palestinian refugees after the 1948 and 1967 wars in the Middle East, fulfilled an important role in aiding Palestinian refugees. Nevertheless, there is also a strong argument that it has supported the Israeli occupation by helping to maintain the post-war status quo. There is also evidence that civil society actors around the world may be co-opted more generally towards state or donor political interests and normative preferences, rather than being connected to local forms of legitimacy. Their aim is to bridge these different elements of politics in order to bring about a socially just and scientifically supportable form of peace.

Since the end of the Cold War numerous forms of conflict resolution, citizen diplomacy, and informal forms of mediation have emerged as a result of civil society actors and their capacities, often supported by international donors in places such as Cyprus, Sri Lanka, Israel/Palestine, and Northern Ireland. As a result, understandings of peace in policy and in practice have begun to include an everyday dimension of peace. This means that it is not enough to have a ceasefire or a peace treaty at the state level, but that society must also be safe to conduct everyday life. NGOs have become important actors in these processes, especially where they provide conflict resolution capacities, early warning of a possible impending conflict, and help construct the institutions necessary for democratization and the rule of law to become integral to an emerging peace.

For example, two London-based organizations, Conciliation Resources and International Alert, work on the premise that the denial of human rights leads to conflict and they support local solutions to conflicts. The Carter Center, based in Atlanta, Georgia (USA), also operates on issues related to democratization, human rights, and conflict resolution. Organizations like International Crisis Group, based in Brussels, seek to report on, advocate, and draw attention to conflicts all over the world. Such organizations often draw on the funding of international donors and work closely with the UN, as well as with local NGOs, governments, and other actors in conflict and post-conflict zones around the world. This points to an alignment between civil, state, and international processes and objectives for peacemaking. It also may be problematic, however, where there are very different goals and cultures, and identities and agendas are overwhelmingly set by the global north.

Organizations such as UNESCO (United Nations Educational, Scientific, and Cultural Organization) also endeavour to connect international peace institutions to the civil peace. It has worked in a range of areas on developing a culture of peace, from education to gender and children's rights.

At the end of the Cold War, a series of UN General Assembly resolutions called for humanitarian assistance to victims of emergencies and natural disasters, for access for accredited agencies, the establishment of relief corridors, and the establishment of the UN Department of Humanitarian Affairs to coordinate humanitarian intervention (though bound to the rules of sovereignty). Furthermore, during the Kurdish crisis in northern Iraq, UN Security Council Resolution 688 of 5 April 1991 facilitated humanitarian intervention involving a number of NGOs. In Bosnia, Security Council Resolution 771 of 13 August 1992 called for humanitarian organizations to have unimpeded access, but it became a point of controversy between the opposing sides in the war. However, during the collapse of the former Yugoslavia in the early 1990s, the international community found it very difficult to offer humanitarian assistance while war was still in process, rapidly becoming overstretched. Similarly, in Somalia, after the collapse of the state in 1991, the UN was supposed to create conditions for the strengthening of civil society and offer humanitarian relief operations. The UN Secretary General's Special Representative attempted to bring in NGOs to facilitate this in order to involve local groups in the peace process, with limited success. Similar patterns of subcontracting essential assistance for civil society were also tried in Haiti, Rwanda, and in Liberia, among many others since the 1990s, with varying degrees of success.

Conclusion

The civil peace has had a significant impact on world affairs. Through it social actors identified processes of violence and first began to organize thinking about how to respond. Civil society has often prepared the scripts for the future development of the IPA when powerful actors have failed to end wars and need new ideas. Their contribution has implied a more positive, hybrid, and everyday form of peace can be created, and also that different societies may have different aspirations or understandings of peace.

It has led to the development of an expanding range of rights and important UN conventions. These included among others the

Declaration of Human Rights in 1948; the Convention on the Prevention and Punishment of the Crime of Genocide in 1948; the Convention on the Political Rights of Women in 1952; the Declaration on the Granting of Independence to Colonial Countries and Peoples in 1960; the International Covenant on Economic, Social, and Cultural Rights in 1966; the Declaration on the Right of Peoples to Peace in 1984; and the United Nations Declaration on the Rights of Indigenous Peoples in 2007. Such conventions were aimed at producing a more positive form of peace in which institutions and states act in the interests of their citizens.

The Millennium Assembly of the UN in 2000 and the Millennium Development Goals followed this logic. The UN agreed to focus on achieving the following goals by the year 2015: eradicating extreme poverty, achieving universal primary education, promoting gender equality and empowering women, reducing child mortality and improving maternal health, combating HIV/AIDS, malaria, and other diseases, and, finally, ensuring environmental sustainability and establishing a global partnership for development. The recent Sustainable Development Goals (2015), and the subsequent Sustaining Peace agenda of the UN have further developed along these lines.

Many other non-governmentally influenced international campaigns have aimed to improve the lot of the peoples of the world. Such civil peace campaigns, in unison with international institutions, have highlighted the importance of avoiding the creation of dependency, being sensitive to the needs of local ownership, and being careful not to offend local or district officials and governments. They adhere to the injunction 'do no harm', often now written into the mandates of various international organizations, while expanding the range of human rights and extending the quality of peace experienced after war.

Such dynamics mean that civil society actors are often described as 'norm entrepreneurs'. They privilege democracy, human rights, and forms of development in their micro-level interventions in society as well as in the realm of international relations. They contribute to a local, grass-roots peace, based upon local community consent and legitimacy in the context of a global, transnational civil society of networks between civil society organizations. The work of OXFAM, Amnesty International, Greenpeace, and many other groups concerned with issues like development and human rights, have contributed to the civil peace.

These organizations have not been uncontroversial. Some commentators argue that NGOs and non-state actors are thinly veiled fronts for powerful state interests, in that they are dependent on state funding and so support state interests, particularly with respect to foreign policy, trade, and the extraction of primary resources. Donor states, agencies, and IFIs generally subcontract work to NGOs precisely because of their access to, and legitimacy within, civil society, and also because humanitarian, social, educational, conflict resolution, and developmental tasks play a significant role in the reconstruction of the state. Sometimes, however, it may be the case that organizations in civil society represent views and groupings opposed to peace, such as those resting on nationalist or sectarian identities or links, or engage in unequal and exploitative relationships with other socio-economic groups in society.

The development and mobilization of the civil peace and its civil society actors has helped alter the nature of the state from one that was often feudal or authoritarian to one that was more democratic, observing the rights of its diverse citizens, and also working for a modicum of equality between them. This also indicates the citizen's capacity to campaign for change and reform at the international level. These developments have enabled a re-envisioning of peace since the latter part of the 20th century. It depends on a range of processes in close association with major donor states (mainly northern states), international organizations like the UN, agencies like the United Nations Development Programme (UNDP) or United Nations High Commission for Refugees (UNHCR), or the World Bank. The World Bank, the Asian Development Bank, and the World Trade Organization, among many others, now encourage state relationships with civil society (even if some critics would argue that unmitigated capitalism undermines civil society at the same time). Overall, this has further enabled the civil peace to develop from the bottom up and from within society.

Recent human security approaches follow this logic. They involve a commitment to a just and sustainable settlement to conflict, the reframing of security debates to include a broader understanding of human security, and the involvement of external non-state actors and indigenous non-state actors. This concept has been widely accepted in key policy circles and in global civil society's interconnected space that links civil society, NGOs, international agencies, and development donors. It was formative of the UN's Sustaining Peace agenda discussions from 2015, which has begun to lay out the groundwork for the theoretical connection of peacemaking approaches with conceptions of justice, in particular global justice.

Chapter 8
The development of an international peace architecture

At the international level, geopolitics and the diplomatic and military balance of power dating back to the Congress of Vienna of 1815, and the Concert of Europe, formed the first stage of an international peace architecture (IPA). These were balancing strategies used by the great powers and statesmen over the course of the 19th century.

The second stage, which emerged at the end of the First World War, attempted to add democracy, self-determination, international law, and organization to the IPA framework, to respond to the obvious limitations of the first stage and the dynamics that had led to the First World War.

The ideological struggle that then marked much of the 20th century between communism and capitalism, and the process of decolonization for the former empires (leading to many new states by the 1960s that expected a place at the international table), represented a third layer of the IPA. It emphasized more substantially the expansion of rights that stage two, relating to human rights, equality, and citizenship, had begun. This development in the architecture also led to demands for more social equality and for a more equal north–south international order.

Such dynamics were also slowly brought into thinking about regional and local peace settlements. They were not present in UN peacekeeping and mediation attempts in the Congo or Cyprus in the 1960s, but by the 1990s they had become more influential in conflict-affected countries such as Cambodia, Democratic Republic of Congo, Sierra Leone, or the Balkans. After the end of the Cold War, the development of stage four emerged, resting on the geopolitical stability provided by the so-called 'unipolar moment'. This stage offered a framework that came to be known as liberal peacebuilding.

Stages five and six of the IPA emerged soon afterwards. Stage five focused on the rebuilding of the state in the context of American hegemony and global capitalism, seeing the state as the main vehicle for peace (whereas liberal peace amplified the role of the UN and international actors in creating checks and balances against war and violence). Stage six is currently in process, and seems to offer two potential paths: the possibility of connecting peace with global justice according to scholarly research findings (including work on global inequality, decolonialism, reconciliation, sustainability, and planetary concerns), or a nationalist retraction that started in stage five from the liberal goals of stage four, perhaps utilizing new technologies of power (digital surveillance and other Orwellian forms).

The evolution of an IPA: layers one to three

The Congress of Vienna and its subsequent 'Concert of Europe' system had maintained a very basic level of negative peace during the 19th century after 1815 between vying imperial powers and states. By the end of the century, reliance on high-level diplomacy for international peace was beginning to look ineffective in the face of the emergence of industrialized modes of warfare, the enormous expansion of trade and technology, and the growing political consciousness of mobilizing masses around the world.

With respect to the latter, along with demands for equality and the vote in newly mobilized populations in the West, the emergence of conscientious objection during the First World War was one of the best-known elements of what was becoming a broader anti-war stance. Conscientious objectors were often imprisoned by the state (in Britain's case) until pacifism became recognized as a legitimate concern of citizens, for whom civilian work could legally be a substitute for active military service. The process that led to this was strongly supported by Cambridge University philosopher Bertrand Russell (1872–1970), who was at various times a liberal, a socialist, and a pacifist.

Campaigns for new forms of world government, to enhance interdependence through trade, and for disarmament, were also significant. The profits and advantages of war were no longer as narrowly understood, as the writings of Norman Angell (1872–1967), a famous anti-war campaigner in the early 20th century, made clear. Both Russell and Angell increased the popular appeal of such ideas.

Prominent businessmen of the era also became involved in promoting world peace, most famously Andrew Carnegie, who used his enormous wealth from the American steel industry in the early 20th century to support trusts and organizations engaged in peace work, as well as funding the construction of the Peace Palace at The Hague. This now houses the International Court of Justice, among other institutions.

The First World War was a great disruption for the various peace movements, but it also allowed their different contributions to begin to coalesce in a second stage of the IPA. After the First World War there emerged a discussion of the value of a liberal and democratic form of peace along with the foundation of the League of Nations. These were the basis for an attempt to build a positive peace through adding a second and more complex framework for peace to the evolving international system. Peace henceforth was to include disarmament, global institutions created to manage conflict, collective action, arbitration over disputes between states, and a Secretariat, as well as a Council whose role it was to enforce the peace. It needed to be internationally organized, given a legal, political, and almost constitutional shape, rather than merely dependent upon luck in the workings of the balance of power by statesmen in their talking shops, as in the 19th century. The understanding of peace was broadening and deepening. A High Commission for Refugees was created to deal with the acute post-war refugee problem. Another institution was to manage the colonial system, which was beginning to collapse because of charges of injustice and because of armed resistance, as well as calls for self-determination from colonial subjects along with the economic and military exhaustion of the colonial powers.

The Treaty of Versailles was shaped by US President Wilson's (1856–1924) 'Fourteen Points', which were intended to make the world 'safe for democracy' through self-determination and consent rather than through domination or occupation. They were remarkably similar to Kant's 'articles' for perpetual peace. However, the US Senate rejected the treaty and the USA did not join the League, though Wilson received the Nobel Peace Prize in 1919 for his efforts.

It very soon became apparent that the first two stages of the IPA, the first aimed at moderating geopolitics and the second at introducing self-determination and liberal democracy, were not enough to deal with newly emerging conflicts during this period. The political mobilization of citizens had been spurred by industrialization, world war, and new ideologies. For example, the foundation of the International Labour Organization (ILO) in 1919 was partly a result of the activism of workers and a growing awareness of the importance of the concept of social justice. The ILO became the first specialized agency of the UN in 1946 and was subsequently to set international standards to mitigate the exploitative dynamics that had so often led to civil conflict. By the 1930s an ideological conflict was brewing that stages one and two of the IPA could not respond to, and would eventually lead to the Cold War after the dead-end of fascism. Social justice considerations spurred a new stage of the IPA after the Second World War, which led to the welfare state as a compromise to hold back the advances of socialism and communism in the West.

Even in the inter-war period, often viewed as the bleakest of epochs marked by financial and political crises, a World Disarmament Conference was convened in 1932. Several major peace movements continued to operate, including the British Peace Pledge Union, the Women's International League for Peace and Freedom, War Resisters International, and various Quaker organizations.

During this period, most famously, Mahatma Gandhi introduced the approaches of *satyagraha* (truth) and *ahimsa* (non-violence), in an attempt to secure India's independence from the British Empire through non-violent methods. These were combined in a non-violent campaign for social justice, development, and equality, hoping to avoid a violent insurgency and civil war. He used these methods to undermine British colonialism in India, but they had a wider impact on the legitimacy of colonialism around the world, rebutting its claim to represent a 'civilizing mission' and exposing its oppressive and racist character. Stage three in the IPA would have to stabilize stages one and two and also deal with both ideological and decolonization dynamics of violence.

In 1932, continuing a long-standing academic engagement with peace, Albert Einstein (1879–1955), well known for developing the general theory of relativity, and Sigmund Freud (1856–1939), the father of psychoanalysis, joined forces to add their intellectual credibility to the various peace movements with an article called 'Why War?' They debated the human capacity to avoid war. Freud wrote,

How long shall we have to wait before the rest of mankind become pacifists too? There is no telling... But one thing we can say: whatever fosters the growth of civilization works at the same time against war.

Einstein returned to the issue in 1955 when he published a manifesto with Bertrand Russell designed to prevent a nuclear conflict, calling on world leaders to seek peaceful solutions to international conflict. It exhorted its readers thus: '[w]e appeal, as human beings, to human beings: Remember your humanity and forget the rest.' Russell himself was later to associate the peace movement with the creation of a world government, as did H. G. Wells (1866–1946), a prolific English writer, socialist, pacifist, and campaigner on social issues.

Consolidation of the international architecture after the Second World War: layers three to four

The new peace that was to follow the war was principally developed according to an American consensus. Cordell Hull (1871–1955), the longest-serving US Secretary of State for President Roosevelt, who received the Nobel Peace Prize in 1945 for his role in establishing the United Nations, introduced a Reciprocal Trade Act in 1934 to open up international trade as a counter to economic nationalism. This was reflected in the Atlantic Charter of 1941 signed by British Prime Minister Winston Churchill and US President Roosevelt, which laid out the internationalist case (though mainly in the global north) for cooperation, free trade, self-determination, decolonization, and the disarmament of aggressive states.

The new peace framework spanned the UN Charter, the emerging Cold War confrontation between the USA and the USSR, and the creation of security, political, and economic arrangements between the USA, the Western industrial countries, and Japan. This system included a military settlement and an institutional framework.

It was developed by a mixture of public and private approaches and organizations, including the US Commission to Study the Basis of a Just and Durable Peace, and the Council for Foreign Affairs, and Britain's Chatham House.

This 'idealist' version of peace engendered in Wilsonianism was now becoming firmly institutionalized in the UN system, which drew together, via an alphabet soup of acronyms, liberal internationalism, self-determination, liberal democracy, and human rights. It was formalized at the conferences of Dumbarton Oaks in 1944 and San Francisco in 1945. Peace had by now come to engender the rejection of interstate war, the provision of humanitarian resources, development, financial regulation and adjustment, and human rights. Though the Security Council was its primary security organization, the UN's specialized agencies, funds, and programmes suggested a much broader view of peace. The World Health Organization, the International Labour Organization, the Food and Agriculture Organization, the UN Development Programme, the World Food Programme, the UN International Children's Emergency Fund, among others, were functional organizations established in order to support a peace resting on social justice. The UN system did not evolve only from the liberal attempt to moderate the victor's peace and its underpinning political realism, but also as a response to the legitimate challenges for social justice, at both a material and ideological level: in other words, in response to the ideological struggle that would soon be known as the Cold War.

Perhaps the most notable statement on peace during this period was Roosevelt's belief that the American Senate's rejection of Wilson's peace in 1920 had been mistaken, and that there was now no turning back from the construction of a liberal international order of democratic states, open markets, and international cooperation. In this order there would be no place for formal imperialism or colonialism.

The International Military Tribunal, set up by the Allies in 1945 to try Nazi war criminals at Nuremberg, provided another important strand of this layer of the IPA. The tribunal had three main jurisdictions, one of which was 'crimes against peace'. Crimes against humanity and war crimes were the most recognized of its jurisdictions, however. The Allies defined a crime against peace as one that involved planning, preparing, or initiating an aggressive war. This soon led to a new wave of legal development with respect to crimes against humanity.

The new system was buttressed by both security guarantees and economic redistribution. NATO played an important military (if only mainly symbolic) role in ensuring that the post-war system would be sustained by a collective security framework (though its capacity to oppose the military power of the Soviet Union was always somewhat questionable). The Truman Doctrine, designed to contain communism in Turkey and Greece, was US President Harry Truman's attempt, from 1947, '...to support free people who are resisting attempted subjugation by armed minorities or by outside pressures'. Marshall Aid (1948-52), a massive American programme named after US Secretary of State George Marshall, was intended to rebuild Europe and prevent the spread of communism.

The 'containment order' which emerged as part of the 1947 Truman Doctrine indicated that there were large parts of the world which would be subject to an alternative, or a more traditional and limited, concept of peace. They would effectively be isolated from the liberal peace both through Western policy and through their compliance with the USSR.

The Declaration of Human Rights in 1947, lobbied for by Eleanor Roosevelt, rapidly became a cornerstone of new thinking and policies. The human rights discourse was derived especially from the work of Western thinkers such as Locke and Mill who put forward the view that individuals have an innate set of rights within the liberal tradition. Implicitly, human rights and peace are equated in much of the literature: one cannot exist without the other. This allowed the UN to base its work on a widely agreed set of standards.

In 1955, the Bandung Conference in Indonesia, attended by 29 newly independent states from the global south including India and Indonesia and representing nearly 1.5 billion people, began a political movement that saw itself as an alternative to the existing post-Cold War order and its inherent instability. Driven by the process of decolonization and related to the ideological struggle and the socialist challenge to Western politics, in 1961, the Non-Aligned Movement formed. It was led by Yugoslavia, Indonesia, India, Egypt, and other states that wanted an alternative approach to politics and development. Briefly at least, it promoted the development of states in the global south as a counterweight to the dominant ideologies of the ongoing Cold War. New voices from the global south were now beginning to enter a debate about the nature of international order, until then mainly dominated by the empires and states of the global north. Thus, stage three of the IPA also had to deal with the claims of former colonial subjects who now sought independence and equality, as made clear in the UN General Assembly by the 1966 Covenant on Economic, Social, and Cultural Rights. Social and transnational movements in the global north continued to make themselves felt by campaigning on issues from disarmament to civil rights, labour, apartheid, and other aspects of social justice. These would henceforth underpin aspirations for a more sophisticated form after the Second World War, as a stage three framework began to emerge for the IPA.

This also illustrated the influence of more critical thinking about peace and development and a range of post-colonial scholars who were by now arguing that the international system required a radical restructuring if inequality and structural violence were to be ended and social justice achieved. Thus, stage three of the architecture challenged the notion of 'basic' human rights, arguing that they needed to be further expanded, and this was connected to the development of social democracy or the welfare state in post-war Europe, as well as to decolonization. This in turn also entailed a substantial attempt to change the nature of the global political economy so that it was more conducive to the development of post-colonial states by the 1970s. After the emergence of the Non-Aligned Movement in the UN General Assembly in the 1960s there followed an attempt to build a New International Economic Order in the 1970s (which was roundly rejected by the West). In addition, the connection of human rights with foreign policy in the Helsinki Final Act of 1974 appeared to consolidate these developments, all with substantial implications for a positive peace agenda.

The peace movement also attracted the attention of US President John F. Kennedy, who said in a speech in Washington in 1963:

> I speak of peace, therefore, as the necessary rational end of rational men ... world peace, like community peace, does not require that each man love his neighbour—it requires only that they live together in mutual tolerance ... our problems are man-made—therefore they can be solved by man.

During this period, United Nations peacekeeping emerged as a new tool to mitigate or prevent conflicts within and between states. It aimed primarily at preventing small conflicts from igniting a superpower conflict. During the period leading up to the collapse of the Soviet Union in 1989–90 both Mikhail Gorbachev, influenced by the Russell–Einstein Manifesto, and US President Ronald Reagan agreed that nuclear wars could not be won and that significant conventional and non-conventional disarmament was required. The anti-nuclear movement had long argued for this cause (as the Campaign for Nuclear Disarmament demonstrated from 1957 onwards).

Another contribution of this era that cemented the institutional framework for peace came from the Geneva Conventions (1949). These extended the earlier treaty in 1864 that established the International Red Cross, as well as standards for international law pertaining to humanitarianism in wartime, the treatment of prisoners, the wounded, and the protection of civilians. International law has been crucial for the institutional peace framework as a set of binding rules between states that provides a stable international order. The International Court of Justice, founded by the UN Charter in 1945, later the European Court of Human Rights, established on the basis of the Council of Europe's 1950 European Convention on Human Rights, and the International Criminal Court, created by the Rome Statute in 2002, were also the results of the evolving institutional peace framework. The development of consent-based governance frameworks at the international and national levels has now produced a significant array of norms, laws, and instruments for peace and justice. In terms of the institutional peace, the body of law about the conduct of war, international humanitarian law, and international human rights law, while slow, cumbersome, and sometimes unenforceable, has been particularly significant.

With these developments it was becoming possible to see the beginnings of the fourth layer of the IPA, which was waiting in the wings for the end of the Cold War. It would enable a much more ambitious system of liberal peacebuilding, and liberal internationalism to emerge.

A regional architecture for peace has also been vital to the developing international architecture. The EU emerged from a post-war attempt to pacify the relationship between the main European states, move away from nationalism, pool resources, and create common goals. It later began to harmonize trade, law, diplomacy, and foreign policy. In 1952 the European Coal and Steel Community was created as the first step towards a European federation, followed by the 1957 Treaty of Rome, which created the European Economic Community and a customs union. Later, the European Union became the most successful regional attempt to maintain peace and order so far. It is a sophisticated successful example of regional conflict resolution and transformation at the social level, as well as constitutional and institutional reform and development, premised upon the stabilization of geopolitics.

A network of other regional organizations is emerging around the world, perhaps most notably the African Union. Established in 2001 as a successor to the Organization of African Unity (founded in 1963), consisting of 54 African states, it aims at promoting solidarity, assisting in political and socio-economic integration and cooperation, as well as supporting security, democracy, human rights, and development.

By this point, the IPA had incorporated responses to geopolitics, through balancing and building up international collaboration in stages one and two. It had also incorporated responses to civil war through democracy, law, and rights in stage two, which also began to formalize international institutions as a response to regional wars. In stage three it had begun to respond to wider justice claims in terms of economics and independence for the industrialized populations of the West and for decolonized states. By mid-century, it was becoming a sprawling edifice, aimed at preventing international, regional, and civil war. It was decentralized, little understood, and difficult to manage, and was expanding rapidly. Yet, the idea of a peace agreement and the practices of peacekeeping by the 1960s were still limited to questions of basic security and power, as the UN missions in Egypt (UNEF 1 and 2, 1956–67 and 1973–9) and the Democratic Republic of the Congo (ONUC, 1960–4) illustrated.

However, the international system now comprised different layers and frameworks and increasingly there was a growing confluence between the aims of social mobilization for more emancipatory forms of peace and the interests of great powers. These forces were to reshape conflict-affected states, at least while they were aligned, inducing reform via pressure from below and above, cemented by a peace agreement. It also provided the basis for the advent of liberal peacebuilding by the end of the century, supported by international actors—mediators, peacekeepers, peacebuilders, donors, and NGOs, which supported civil society and state reform. They were now supported by many of the dominant peacebuilding actors, agencies, and states, such as the UN, World Bank, or key donors like the USA, UK, Japan, or the EU.

Peace after the Cold War

By the end of the century the international peacebuilding architecture was focused on redesigning the international and states-system, and enabling civil society in the context of scientific advances, and on the governance of the global economy.
It incorporated a very powerful critique desiring social justice, implying much greater international equality was required.
It pointed to even wider notions of global justice and sustainability. As Kant inferred long ago in the 17th century, social justice requires global justice. Yet, this architecture is also subject to numerous international contradictions, it is very complex, inter-generational, and requires substantial material support from diverse constituencies, and populations who are required to act in solidarity with others in distant war-torn countries.

After the collapse of the Soviet Union, the liberal peace became, for the West at least, the leading response to conflict, war, and violence. An awareness of the global, regional, state, and local dynamics of peace, and its social, economic, political, and cultural dimensions, had now coalesced around the benefits of democracy and capitalism, some social welfare on the part of the state, and an international architecture of peace and development led by the UN. UN Conventions, documents, committees, agencies, and organizations now began to emerge and focus on improving the local, state, and global dynamics of social, political, economic, and institutional aspects of peace. The most important of these were *An Agenda for Peace* in 1992, the Cairo Population Summit of 1992, the Rio de Janeiro 'Earth Summit' of 1992, the Beijing Women's Summit of 1995, the UN Millennium Declaration of 2000, and *Responsibility to Protect* in 2005. Together all of these developments contributed to stage four of the evolution of the IPA.

Stage four was perhaps the most successful stage of the architecture yet, in that it stabilized the previous stages and offered a concrete strategy for dealing with post-Cold War conflicts, though it was not without its limitations. It provided a platform for a convergence of peacemaking, peacekeeping, peacebuilding, development, state reform, international institutionalization and law, social movements, and civil society actors. Liberal, internationalist, idealist, and pacifist movements, associated with humanitarianism, the formation of international institutions like the UN, international law, democracy, free trade, and forms of economic redistribution, were at the forefront of what appeared to be popular mobilization and non-violent strategies aimed at a wider peace.

Thus, liberal peace incorporated a diverse array of aspects. Once security is assured (a negative peace) the next stage is to create a positive peace. A ceasefire, disarmament, demilitarization, and demobilization, was crucially important in the first instance, followed by a viable political settlement and state reform.

This stage also saw the elevation of voices from the global south, along with a range of what might be called 'subaltern' actors: women's groups, marginalized identity groups, the poor and disadvantaged, and many others. They also slowly built up their local and global networks of advocacy in local society, the state, and international institutions, demanding expanded rights for identity, equality, justice, and reconciliation, as well as security and development. They added to the chorus and activities relating to the reform of the old warlike (often patriarchal) sovereignties of empire or state. Long-standing racist, patriarchal, and colonial understandings of peace, and even more sophisticated versions based on liberal internationalism, have gradually broadened.

War was becoming increasingly undermined as a political tool except where there were significant threats against the international community, or for humanitarian reasons, to overthrow occasional renegade and terrorist-supporting regimes, as in Bosnia, Sierra Leone, or Afghanistan and Iraq. That is not to say that it was absent, as shown by the recent and extended wars in Syria and Yemen, or the so-called 'hybrid war' (which includes traditional warfare, irregular warfare, and cyber tactics) as used by Russia in Syria or Ukraine, amongst others in the 2010s. Such 'innovation' in warfare, however, normally led to innovation in the international peace architecture.

Thus, the UN continued to develop its capacity for peace along with the expanding donor system. International law was increasingly taken seriously even if not enforced. Nuclear and other disarmament became internationally accepted. Expectations about peace also now included issues relating to civil society, human rights, gender, development, and extended into research and education. Policymaking on peace, development, security, rights, and needs advanced significantly, even if the redress of direct or structural violence has so far been uneven. Concepts like human security (as opposed to state security) became part of the institutional agenda in the UN system in the 1990s, emphasizing the human consequences of conflict and dimensions of peace. All of these elements of the IPA meant it had become the most complex and effective framework for peace ever seen.

Such complexity entailed substantial cost, risks, and needed heavyweight leadership, not to mention political will, which in practice was only intermittently provided by the USA.

Into the 21st century: layers five to six

Variations on the liberal peace also began to emerge by the 2000s, often supported by the newer actors and organizations, the emerging countries and a range of local and transnational actors, on the world stage. Most recognized states play a role in various international organizations—from the UN to the IMF, World Bank, European Union, Organization for Security and Cooperation in Europe (OSCE), the AU, and many other regional organizations—that contribute to peace, development, and security in the many parts of today's world where war has occurred or still threatens. At the elite or state level diplomats and international officials utilize tools such as negotiation, mediation, conflict resolution, peacebuilding, statebuilding, or development processes. International peacekeepers' military, peacekeeping, and humanitarian intervention may provide a platform for these tools. Peace in positive or even hybrid form is a local and international, collective aspiration, even if a 'will to power' (implying at best a negative peace) has often captured the world's headlines.

By the 2000s after problems with liberal peacebuilding in Cambodia, Bosnia, and other cases around the world, and with the advent of the War on Terror, statebuilding shifted the focus for peacebuilding from human rights and democracy back towards regional security. This was a stage five response to the new synergies between civil war and terrorism that were emerging, especially in the Middle East. This appeared to be a regressive step for the IPA, as seen in Iraq after 2004, as it focused mainly on regional security, the stabilization of the state as the vehicle of domestic and international order, and matters of trade as opposed to rights and democracy. On paper, the UN, global civil society, and scholars were already developing a stage six as a response to heightened nationalism, populism, inequality, injustice, and unsustainability, as well as to the disruptions caused by hybrid forms of war and violence as well as new technologies and their applications for violence. This led by the 2010s to discussions about the Sustainable Development and Sustaining Peace agendas (2015/18).

The overall international architecture has evolved via the work of many often disconnected groups over the centuries as an inter-generational, multifaceted response to the changing problems of war. Multiple layers of peace praxis have been placed upon previous layers to deal with each new type of war, and have been embedded in social, state, and international organization, networks, law, and institutions. They have always emerged as a response to the last war, after the event, and have a limited predictive capacity. The techniques and underpinning systems of war always seem to be far ahead. The overall structure of the IPA is politically and scientifically complex, under-resourced and expensive to maintain, ambitious, and thus fragile. It is at risk of collapse if a new layer (layer six) cannot stabilize the previous layers or respond to new and emerging types of conflict quickly enough.

Chapter 9
Peacekeeping, peacebuilding, and statebuilding

As the liberal peace coalesced in modern international relations in the fourth stage of the development of an IPA, there emerged different approaches, which are examined in this chapter. These involved a range of processes designed to manage, resolve, or transform conflict:

(a) Peacekeeping, diplomacy, and mediation: a first generation approach aimed at a negative peace, from the 1950s onwards (created during the 1956 Suez Crisis), in which neutral military intervention brought about ceasefires often through the UN;

(b) Civil society efforts: a second generation approach from the late 1960s more focused on law, rights, social reconciliation, and a positive peace;

(c) by the 1990s, a third generation of approaches focused on building liberal peace through bringing together development, peacekeeping, peacebuilding, statebuilding, democratization, creating a rule of law, promoting human rights, civil society, and capitalism. This also offered a positive form of peace;

(d) a fourth generation approach, still developing, which combines the liberal peace with a recognition of local and contextual peace traditions. This may produce positive hybrid forms of peace.

Conflict management after the Second World War: international mediation and peacekeeping

The thinking that underlies the victor's peace contributed to modern 'conflict management' approaches, which aimed at maintaining a negative peace. This represented a first generation of attempts to manage international conflict and stabilize the international system during the Cold War. However, during this period, most wars were barely addressed by such tools, and instead were fought to a conclusion (such as in the Korean war 1950–3). Conflict management approaches have sometimes included the use of force by coalitions of states, but more often tools such as UN peacekeeping, high-level diplomacy (meaning the involvement of senior politicians, statesmen and women, and international bureaucrats like the UN Secretary General), and the use of international mediation. Such processes often produced 'zero-sum' outcomes in which a negative peace consisted of unstable relations between 'winners' and 'losers' in a conflict. Such de-escalation was useful during the Cold War, when nuclear conflict between the superpowers was always plausible.

To this effect, the UN Charter stated:

> All Members shall settle their international disputes by peaceful means in such a manner that international peace and security, and justice, are not endangered.

> The parties to any dispute, the continuance of which is likely to endanger the maintenance of international peace and security, shall, first of all, seek a solution by negotiation, enquiry, mediation, conciliation, arbitration, judicial settlement, resort to regional agencies or arrangements, or other peaceful means of their own choice.

These binding statements are central to any modern conception of conflict management, aimed at maintaining international security. Negative peace during much of the Cold War involved the preservation of the territorial integrity of states, often after decolonization or after a proxy war between the USA and the USSR (although many wars during this period received no such treatment, as with the Vietnam War from 1955 and its outcome in 1975, because the superpowers were involved). The human rights of citizens were of secondary importance at best.

Reaching a ceasefire agreement, withdrawing foreign forces, establishing law and order, and achieving a comprehensive peace agreement at the diplomatic level were the key components of conflict management approaches, following closely the first stage in the IPA and its tradition of geopolitical balancing and the maintenance of the existing states system. It aimed at supporting a basic minimum order without any overt violence. To achieve this any third parties involved in mediation or peacekeeping had to be neutral and impartial or, alternatively, work according to their power and interests. International mediation as a diplomatic activity required interactions between states over territory, alliances, constitutional agreements, or boundaries, often led by a leader or by the UN. As mediation became more sophisticated, according to William Zartman (a professor of political science at Johns Hopkins University), it enabled the search for windows of opportunity provided by 'hurting stalemates' (where disputants are caught up in a painful situation where they could not win on the battlefield but neither could they afford to give up the struggle) and 'ripe moments' (where new opportunities arise for a settlement to occur). The disputants might be more likely to settle and mediators, diplomats, and peacekeeping operations would be able to mobilize.

Though not mentioned by name in the UN Charter, UN peacekeeping was probably the most innovative of modern conflict management approaches, but it still reflected the close control of UN Security Council members of international matters and was not designed to settle a conflict. Peacekeeping was developed by the UN Secretary General and his team in 1956 during the Suez Crisis in order to prevent it from sparking a major conflict between the superpowers.

This early type of peacekeeping involved four main principles: that the force should be defensive rather than offensive; that it should not include troops drawn from major powers (to enhance its neutrality); that it should be impartial; and that it should have consent and not intervene in the dispute. In this way a small and symbolic force, cheaply run, could offer symbolic support for peace and security, help uphold the UN Charter, and not take great risks because it had the consent of the parties to the dispute, whether the superpowers in the UN Security Council or armies and guerrilla fighters on the ground. It could also provide a calmer environment in which peace talks might be held.

The earliest forms of peacekeeping were essentially observer missions or disengagement missions (as in the missions in Kashmir in 1947 or the Middle East in 1948), but they quickly developed into forms intended to provide the conditions of stability in which diplomacy, mediation, and negotiation could begin alongside peacekeeping forces (as in Cyprus from 1964 onwards). This was a response to the long-term problems of geopolitics, which ultimately, as with stages two and three of the IPA, require political settlements to be mediated and the aspirations of society to be met. Many of the peacekeeping missions since 1956, and the Suez Crisis (1956–7), aimed at facilitating independence of colonial territories, enabling colonial powers to withdraw while saving face. They were aimed at preventing small wars, as in Cyprus in 1963 or 1974, from escalating into major conflicts. They normally patrolled agreed ceasefires, and tried to oversee the withdrawal of troops and create conditions in which a peace agreement might be plausible, as after the Suez Crisis in 1956 or in Cyprus from 1964. In other words they tried to support a negative peace, but soon realized that more was required if the conflict was not to flare up upon their departure.

After the end of the Cold War many conflicts did flare up, in the Balkans, Africa, Central America, and Africa. UN peacekeeping again endeavoured to implement the terms of prior peace agreements negotiated by the UN Secretary General or other international mediators in places such as Namibia (1989–90), where an agreement between South Africa and local leaders led to Namibian Independence overseen by the UN. There were also similar UN forces sent around this time to implement agreements which brought civil wars to an end in Angola and Mozambique. Observer missions also monitored the transition into peace after the end of civil wars in Nicaragua and El Salvador.

More ambitious missions also occurred, as in Cambodia where the UN also acted as a transitional government during the process of building a democracy (1992–3). They became more involved in building a liberal form of peace. By the late 1990s and under increasing pressure, the UN was trying to conduct peacekeeping without clear local consent, as in Bosnia-Herzegovina, exposing peacekeepers and international staff to the risk of being drawn into the conflict rather than being perceived as neutral third parties.

The evolution of peacekeeping occurred because the practice of conflict management in places like DR Congo or Cyprus in the early 1960s had failed to cope with the weaknesses of a negative peace or respond to local demands for a positive peace. Early forms of peacekeeping achieved some mitigation of open violence but rarely a comprehensive peace settlement (perhaps with the exception of the Camp David Accords between Israel and Egypt after wars in 1967 and 1973, though this was mediated with some persuasiveness by US President Carter in 1978). Negative peace suffered from the same weakness as the victor's peace: it needed permanent military and material guarantees, otherwise any peace process it engendered might collapse. This evolution highlighted the significance of further innovation in the IPA.

Peace through conflict resolution

A second generation attempt to address the underlying dynamics of conflict, and to resolve and reconcile conflicting parties, focused on the rights and needs of citizens rather than states. This reflected broader developments in stages two and three in the IPA.

It aimed at creating a 'win–win' outcome (where all parties felt they had won as a result of the peace process) driven by responding to the needs of civil society in particular. It focused on the root causes of conflict from the perspective of individuals, groups, and societies, and on mutual accommodation. It is often described as 'track II', track I being formal diplomacy, mediation, and negotiation. From this perspective, conflict arises out of a repression of basic human needs and is a social as well as a psychological phenomenon. Second generation approaches saw injustice as a source of social unrest and human needs offered a framework for understanding the causes of conflict, how it might be resolved, and how reconciliation and justice could be achieved, rather than merely managing enmity. This civil society-oriented discourse aimed to construct a positive peace addressing the societal roots of conflict and discriminatory and inequitable social, economic, and political structures.

From this theoretical basis a number of new methods for peacemaking emerged. Citizen diplomacy, conflict resolution, and similar track II approaches became common from the 1990s in places such as Cyprus, the Middle East, Northern Ireland, or Sri Lanka as an alternative and innovative way to reconcile societies. Informal 'back channels' were created between a range of political and informal civil society actors across conflict lines. Meetings often took place between social groups to discuss local matters and how to improve everyday life, as well as to discuss broader visions of a peace process. Informal channels of communication often facilitated a peace process at the official level and improved security significantly.

This was particularly successful in Northern Ireland when the peace process began after 1994. It took place at both the elite and the social level, and was cemented by massive civil society and economic investment from the British government and the EU to iron out structural and economic inequalities between its communities. There was also a parallel agreement between the main governments involved and the creation of new and improved political institutions (the Good Friday Agreement of 1998). However, the potential of these approaches in other locations such as Israel/Palestine and Sri Lanka was not realized despite some promise in the 1990s. Their peace processes reverted to nationalistic, power-driven, formal processes, and eventually were not able to overcome the usual problems associated with sovereignty, territorialism, militarization, and nationalism. Conflict resolution approaches have, however, made it clear that in any society a peace process should meet political, social, and economic needs and rights. It was also an essential contribution to the emerging fourth layer of the IPA.

Conflict transformation, peacebuilding, and statebuilding

This approach was soon augmented by conflict transformation theory, which argued for a process that transforms the relationships, interests, and nature of state and society which feed a conflict. This is a long-term and multidimensional process, aimed at addressing the roots of conflict, including perceptions, communications, inequality, and social injustice. Liberal peacebuilding was heavily indebted to such approaches, in that it was soon realized that a more ambitious process such as conflict transformation would require more complex peace processes. After 1990, liberal peacebuilding involved large-scale and external forms of intervention, in countries like Cambodia, Bosnia, Sierra Leone, Timor-Leste, Afghanistan, and many others.

There were varying estimates, but by its recent peak in 2008 about 110,000 personnel were deployed in conflict or post-conflict countries populated by a total of 100 million people. These operations include a range of components, such as military intervention, democratization, and development, managed by international organizations such as the UN and the World Bank, foreign donors, and many regional and international agencies. They aimed to build a positive peace in liberal capitalist and democratic form, and focused on security, democracy, human rights, the rule of law, development, free trade, and a vibrant civil society.

Stage four in the IPA reframed geopolitical balancing, peacekeeping, mediation, and peace processes to expand liberal democracy, capitalism, and international law across the world as a solution to civil and regional wars of various types. Liberal peacebuilding linked peace and security directly with development, democracy, the rule of law, human rights, and a vibrant civil society in a modern state framework. This is embedded in a system of global governance, international law, and trade.

This top-down architecture only offered part of the picture, however. Peacebuilding was initially theorized in the peace research literature as a grass-roots, bottom-up process in which a local consensus within society led to a positive peace, representing the earlier claims for self-determination, welfare, and development that had emerged with stages two to four of the IPA. As the concept evolved, it came to represent a convergence with the agendas of human rights, development, democratization, and human security, and in practice it also had to bring together conflicting interests of major states in the UN Security Council after the end of the Cold War. It was in part based upon the development of more ambitious and integrated forms of peacekeeping, which evolved rapidly from multidimensional forms at first with the consent of local actors and in a multilateral form, and then, on occasion, without their consent. As a result, the demands on the role of the UN and its supporting actors multiplied and diversified enormously in terms of the tasks they undertook to build peace and the many locations around the world where they did so.

A number of UN documents, starting with *An Agenda for Peace* in 1992, described this new stage in the IPA in detail. This UN document, akin to a Cold War peace settlement, described peacebuilding as 'action to identify and support structures which will tend to strengthen and solidify peace in order to avoid a relapse into conflict'. In 2007 the UN Secretary General provided a comprehensive definition:

> Peacebuilding involves a range of measures targeted to reduce the risk of lapsing or relapsing into conflict by strengthening national capacities at all levels for conflict management, and to lay the foundations for sustainable peace and development. Peacebuilding strategies must be coherent and tailored to specific needs of the country concerned, based on national ownership, and should comprise a carefully prioritized, sequenced, and therefore relatively narrow set of activities aimed at achieving the above objectives.

However, this approach was constrained by geopolitical concerns, the need to consider sovereign states and their right of non-intervention, as well as its implicit claim that peace should be built according to a universal formula. As with peacekeeping from the 1960s, most peacebuilding operations in the 1990s took place in the global south. This gave the impression that northern countries were pacifying disadvantaged populations rather than responding to more substantive political claims for security (often meaning human security), justice, and development.

Since the early 1990s UN Integrated Missions have endeavoured to support the broad ambitions of peacebuilding, as in the Balkans in the early 1990s along with other actors (such as NATO, the EU, and the OSCE). The early post-Cold War peacekeeping operations in Namibia, Cambodia, Angola, Mozambique, and El Salvador seemed to offer the hope that the peace engendered by UN intervention could go beyond patrolling ceasefires and would instead contribute to the democratization and liberal reform of failing and failed states. This blueprint was also used in Cambodia, Bosnia, Kosovo, Sierra Leone, Liberia, DR Congo, and East Timor and others during the 1990s and 2000s. Liberal peacebuilding came to represent a multilevel approach, attempting to address the local, state, and regional aspects of, and actors in, conflict. It became multidimensional in nature in that it brought together a wide range of actors who were able to deal with a wide range of issues and dynamics. As the concept of security expanded so too emerged pressure for international law and human rights to expand further than their 1940s version.

The record has been mixed. Many operations in different locations resulted in authoritarian regimes and a significant percentage have failed. This was because the process was inconsistent in its design, was inefficient and ill coordinated by international actors, thus losing localized legitimacy with conflict-affected populations. Deficiencies also arose because local elites blocked peace processes in order to defend their interests, even if it meant stalemate or war.

To avoid such tendencies, international administration of post-conflict environments (meaning that the UN or specific groups of states assume responsibility) became more common in the 1990s and 2000s. This approach was used in Bosnia-Herzegovina, Kosovo, and Timor-Leste. In Afghanistan and Iraq in the 2000s, more coercive approaches were used, prioritizing regional and international stability and reforming the state (a process often now called 'statebuilding'). Both approaches only achieved a negative peace if at all.

Peacebuilding approaches drew upon the idea that peace can be built by external actors such as the UN, donors, NGOs, and foreign militaries, based on liberal norms to create a liberal state. By the start of the 21st century, an even more ambitious agenda emerged via the *Millennium Development Goals* (2000) and a doctrine called the *Responsibility to Protect* (2005). This implied that sovereignty entailed responsibility for citizens, and if a state undermined the human rights of its citizens, committed acts of genocide, war crimes, crimes against humanity, and ethnic cleansing, the international community might intervene. These trajectories kept developing, with the 2015 UN Sustainable Development Goals, and its subsequent Sustaining Peace agenda (2018), incorporating new knowledge about local legitimacy and sustainability into peace frameworks.

In sum liberal peacebuilding continued the shift towards a positive understanding of peace, to which end the UN Peacebuilding Commission was established in 2005. Working in countries such as Burundi, Sierra Leone, Guinea Bissau, and the Central African Republic, the UN Peacebuilding Commission, Peacebuilding Fund, and Peacebuilding Support Office were involved in integrating and coordinating the range of processes that peacebuilding involved.

Liberal peacebuilding was widely criticized for resting on military intervention, being inefficient, and ill coordinated, for assuming that promoting democracy, human rights, and trade were enough to make peace, and for not paying enough attention to local preferences and needs. On average, many peace settlements during this period remained partially unimplemented or frozen, though improvements in peace and security around the world were achieved. Such approaches were also resisted by states such as Russia and China, among others, on the grounds that they undermined their own regional interests (such as Russia's influence in the Balkans), represented northern/Western hegemony, and were an attack on sovereignty. By the 2000s, such countries were developing their own peacekeeping, peacebuilding, and development strategies. Most notable, perhaps, was China's 'Belt and Road' project to connect China with developing markets and to stabilize them in China's interests via debt dependency and authoritarian capitalism (as opposed to liberal democracy).

Statebuilding

In the early 2000s, a new doctrine called statebuilding emerged, which represented a significant retreat from the normative aspirations of the liberal peace (relating to human rights in particular). It focused on the basic security and economic functions of the state. It represented a fifth stage in the development of the IPA, the first stage which involved a retreat from the expanding norms and rights that had previously been associated with liberal peacebuilding. Increasing state weaknesses in the areas of security, crime, and terrorism were seen as the main threats to international peace and security, especially in relation to states like Afghanistan, Somalia, North Korea, Pakistan, and others. Such failing and post-conflict states had become breeding grounds for a dangerous mix of terrorism, poverty, crime, trafficking, and humanitarian catastrophe, which might have spilt over into other states.

The aim of statebuilding was to create prosperous and stable liberal states framed by a 'good governance' agenda, via externalized strategies of intervention. Statebuilding was designed to produce an intervention with a small or 'light footprint'—as in Afghanistan before the 2021 withdrawal of American forces—rather than a form of trusteeship. According to a 1997 World Bank report, 'The State in a Changing World', this type of state framework should have a set of core functions, ranging from the minimalist functions of security, law, and order, to the 'activist' functions associated with legitimate institutions, public services, welfare, and social support. Statebuilding was assumed to capture both local and international forms of legitimacy and especially the local desire for sovereignty and modernization. Its genealogy reached back to the more substantial reconstruction and nation-building experiments after the US civil war, in Germany and Japan, and much of Western Europe after the Second World War. Statebuilding was favoured by the USA after the 9/11 attacks but suffered serious flaws: a lack of a peace dividend and a failure to improve security, everyday peace, or social justice, as graphically illustrated in contemporary Afghanistan and Iraq.

Assessing recent achievements

Liberal peacebuilding and statebuilding represent the most advanced Western and global consensus on the importance of international institutions and open markets, and on democracy and human rights, in preventing conflict as well as attending to its underlying causes. Stage four in the IPA seemed to stabilize the previous layers and offer concrete potential for ending war more substantially. There was, however briefly, a wide-ranging consensus also including non-Western states (though non-developed and subaltern actors were less represented). It had some success in reducing violence and inducing some compliance with liberal norms, institutions, law, and markets. Yet there have been few outright 'successes' to speak of, partly because the peace dividend was weak, cultural norms were not recognized, and nationalism and territorialism were maintained because the IPA still depended on state-centric systems and approaches. Peace settlements, statebuilding, and peacebuilding have tended to lead to a negative peace. The number of interstate and civil wars have been reduced, as have the number of deaths, however. Thus, this is at least a basis for a more positive peace to emerge.

However, many of the UN attempts at democratization since the end of the Cold War suffered some form of authoritarian regime within several years. Many peace processes stagnated or became frozen during the stage five engagement with statebuilding, during which the international community lost impetus and focused more on questions affecting northern states' security, particularly with the onset of the War on Terror. In addition, international financial institutions like the World Bank and International Monetary Fund used structural adjustment and development projects that failed to provide the sorts of economic opportunities and welfare that would be expected to provide a quick 'peace dividend'. The relationship between peacebuilding and justice has also been controversial. Justice often remained subservient to stability, particularly because stage five moved human rights into a secondary category, and some influential individuals and organizations in conflict environments continued to be implicated in violence, corruption, or crimes against humanity. In effect, liberal peacebuilding and statebuilding became systems of governance rather than processes of justice, reconciliation, and restitution.

There have been several common complaints:

(i) that there are not enough resources available;

(ii) that there was a lack of local capacity, skill, participation, or consent;

(iii) that there was a lack of coordination and too much duplication amongst the international actors;

(iv) that the process was mainly owned by international actors rather than by its recipients;

(v) that the issues that face society in social and welfare terms were ignored;

(vi) that peacebuilding and statebuilding were mainly driven by neoliberal marketization and development agendas rather than reconciliation;

(vii) that it perpetuated local and international inequality and elite predation.

Over time blockages to peacekeeping, international mediation, conflict resolution, and transformation, as well as peacebuilding and statebuilding, have grown. Blocking tactics may evolve into more concerted attempts at spoiling a peace process. Such counter-peace strategies have become embedded in many peace processes, intractable conflicts, and frozen conflicts around the world, as in Cyprus, Abkhazia, Bosnia, and Kosovo, and many others.

Despite the promise of stage four of the IPA, what emerged with stage five were fragile states across conflict-affected regions such as the Caucasus or the Balkans, propped up by weakened international actors, from the UN, the World Bank, to national donors or international NGOs. However, much had been learned about peacebuilding through such experiences, including the need for locally legitimate systems of authority, political and economic frameworks, society, religion, and culture to be part of any framework for peace. Hybrid forms of peace and political order were now beginning to emerge as a response.

Chapter 10
Hybrid forms of peace, peace formation, and counter-peace

In a step beyond liberal peace frameworks, hybrid forms of peace have emerged in diverse locations around the world. They represent a platform on which a stage six layer of the IPA is being built, pointing in sum to the incorporation of issues of historical injustice, global inequality, and long-term sustainability into peace processes and related activities (as identified in the UN's recent Sustaining Peace Agenda (2018)). Local patterns of politics based on everyday, contextual social, cultural, and historical norms, identities, and material resources influence peace along with Western/northern peace approaches. Hybrid political order and hybrid peace is formed through political contestation involving a range of actors, their preferences, and security interests. In some cases, a negative hybrid peace may be emerging.

An everyday form of peace is its objective, complementing the liberal peace that emerged from the internationalist dreams of the 20th century. It raises the question—in an era when the West is no longer internationally dominant—of how local forms of legitimacy, or alternative political, social, and economic systems, and norms of peace can engage with international forms. Can international understandings of a liberal human rights regime (part of the civil peace and crucial to a liberal social contract) be reconciled with local, customary, or religious practices in very diverse locations around the world? How can the material demands for a peace dividend be met after war in this context? A hybrid form of peace may therefore be more localized and networked, but it also has to deal with the very significant global inequalities that remain between states and societies around the world.

Hybrid political orders

Hybrid forms of peaceful political order, especially in intractable and frozen conflicts and blocked peace processes, are widespread. This is especially in those cases arising since the end of the Second World War, from the Korean Peninsula to the Middle East, the Balkans, or Colombia. In Somalia, despite the collapsed nature of the state, many local communities have organized themselves to maintain stability, justice, and the economy through customary and ad hoc informal institutions, as notably in Puntland and Somaliland. In Timor-Leste, as in Liberia, Mozambique, Sierra Leone, Guatemala, the Solomon Islands, and many others, international and local cooperation has produced a specifically contextual version of peace, to varying degrees incorporating customary practices.

There is the potential for positive hybrid forms, as in Timor-Leste or Sierra Leone, where local customary law and governance may be slowly reshaping and aligning with the modern state. Local organizations, operating in civil society, often informally, and combining local customs and justice with the emerging modern state, have been vital to this process, though elites may also resist the required reforms and compromises. Thousands of internationally supported local development committees and NGOs have been essential to this process. It may require, as in Afghanistan, difficult compromises with tribal groups and their historical practices, including the Taliban and various warlords, which would certainly involve significant reform on their part too. The risk—as in Afghanistan—is that it slides into failure rather than a positive peace outcome. In Cambodia a negative outcome has been the emergence of an authoritarian democracy, though a vibrant civil society, particularly in the realms of human rights, has kept pressure on the government. In Bosnia-Herzegovina, the conditions of a weak, post-war state have only been partially alleviated by both international support and local communities' attempts at mitigating them, but there has been an acute risk of the Dayton Agreement of 1995 collapsing over the last decade.

However, this concept capitalizes on the core of the conflict resolution, transformation, and peacebuilding agendas. It addresses human needs and root causes, connecting the new state or polity with older, locally recognizably legitimate agendas and engages with grass roots and the most marginalized members of post-conflict polities and their political, social, cultural, and economic claims. Whether this provides a basis for a positive form of hybrid peace to emerge, or a frozen conflict and a negative form of hybrid peace, depends on the development of the overall IPA and political will to further refine it.

Recent attempts to refine international policies have followed this line of thought over the last decade, most notably with the UN's Sustainable Development Goals (2015) and the Sustaining Peace agenda (2017), presaging a new stage six in the IPA. These documents point to the significance of the relationship between global justice, sustainability, local legitimacy, and the overall IPA.

Local contributions and everyday peace

Local groups have often formed to bring about peace for themselves on a small and now widely replicated scale. Everyday forms of peace centre around the small things individuals and groups can do to de-escalate and avoid local conflict in their everyday lives, which over time might lead to more ambitious social and political peacemaking strategies. For example, in the 1990s conflict resolution workshops run in Cyprus by mainly American or European scholars allowed Cypriots, many of whom had long preferred accommodation and pluralism on the island to nationalism and violence, to meet across the militarized buffer zone, which had divided Greek and Turkish Cypriots since 1974 or even earlier. Despite problems, local participants were able to use the process to build a wider peace constituency, which allowed a sophisticated form of everyday coexistence to emerge amongst the members of these 'inter-communal groups'. By the 2000s, formal peacemaking attempts recognized the importance of such civil society movements, after years of ignoring their potential, and they even gained their own building in the bufferzone, which has hosted an array of political, social, and cultural activities. However, their impact on the political process has been limited in recent times.

In Mozambique and Namibia, since the end of their conflicts in the 1990s, governments or internationals have not addressed social and economic issues fully, given the history of colonization and white settlement. Civil society is often described as weak or absent, dependent upon fickle donor priorities and funds. Nevertheless, local organizations have continued to engage in human rights, development, education, or training work, often within a subsistence context (meaning they do not receive any donor or international support). In Mozambique, one NGO uses traditional musical instruments in rural areas to teach people about pluralism, peace, and coexistence. Another organization developed its own small arms decommissioning project, which earned worldwide fame. Weapons are turned into sculptures and pieces of art, such as *The Throne of Weapons*, made by the Mozambican artist Cristovao Canhavato from decommissioned weapons collected after the end of the civil war in 1992. Such small activities often have a broader social significance even if political and economic obstacles to peace remain. Their ambitions are captured in a famous sculpture outside the UN Building in New York (see Figure 8).

In Guatemala, a prosperous European settler community has dominated politics and the economy before and even since the

8. Non-violence—*The Knotted Gun* (1980) is a bronze sculpture by Swedish artist Carl Fredrik Reuterswärd which is placed outside the UN Building in New York.

peace process of the 1990s. The majority community of Mayan people often live in rural settings in relative poverty. They have developed numerous ways of preserving their culture and identity and have increasingly become more successful in finding spaces in which they can survive and coexist with the modern state, as well as to have their culture and cosmology included in national and international fora.

In Sri Lanka, despite very difficult circumstances for any peace process during the 2000s, certain local organizations such as the National Peace Council have navigated around the problems of separatist violence, nationalism and majoritarianism, and ethnic and religious chauvinism. The organization, among others, has supported rights and pluralism and with skill that other internationals, such as mediators from countries like Norway, foreign donors, or the UN, have not been able to emulate. While the latter have been undermined by rapacious local politics, local organizations, working in the areas of human rights and peacebuilding, have managed to maintain their roles of advocacy and accountability despite difficult, changing local conditions.

In both Kosovo and Bosnia-Herzegovina after the wars and during the late 1990s and early 2000s, international actors became frustrated with their local counterparts' tendencies to obstruct institutional reforms designed to bring the liberal state into being, particularly where these demanded social, cultural, political, and economic, reform. The result in Bosnia was deadlock over the reform of the state while in Kosovo it brought into being a contested state. In Bosnia a number of civil society organizations on the ground, involved in human rights and transitional justice matters and cultural projects, emerged in an attempt to speed up progress in resolving the country's various problems (though not necessarily conforming to international expectations of a liberal peace). In Kosovo, a range of organizations had undertaken to provide many of the services that the state had refused them during the 1980s, and after the war in 1999 they emerged from

9. These buildings are known as *uma lulik* or sacred houses in Timor-Leste.

the shadows to become part of the new state. Both phenomena denote a potential hybrid form of peace and state emerging from localized, everyday processes.

In Timor-Leste since independence in 2002 and during the UN peacekeeping operation and especially after the recurrence of violence in 2006, local actors have been crucial in building a hybrid peace that has both social and political dimensions. Two of the most visible examples were the return to the landscape of 'sacred houses' and the creation of a social welfare system. Sacred houses are centres of family and social life, where local politics, arrangements, and economic support are decided, and where celebrations and ceremonies take place that bind communities, including conflict resolution ceremonies (see Figure 9). Their re-emergence is indicative of a deeper stabilization where international approaches had failed.

In other cases, such as the Solomon Islands, similar dynamics emerged. Most communities gain their law and justice, representation, and welfare from localized, customary, or church-oriented institutions and processes. The modern state appears to them to be distant and often predatory, as do international markets. Similarly, Afghanistan's former President Hamid Karzai developed his 'big tent' strategy to try to be inclusive of difficult actors such as the Taliban and a range of factions after the war from 2001. However, these attempts at creating states that were more inclusive of powerful actors as well as a broad range of civil actors have had mixed results. In Afghanistan, it led to its co-option by warlords, and in many other cases, authoritarian outcomes have emerged.

In all of these cases, the growing role of Chinese and Russian interests over the last 20 years has also played a role in both supporting a weak state and diverting it away from human rights-based approaches. In turn, this has deflected hybrid forms of peace away from establishing a relationship between the state, everyday legitimacy, and human rights, towards authoritarian models which are often populist in nature, as has also been seen since the 2007 war in Sri Lanka.

Encouragingly for liberal peacebuilding's supporters, however, civil society actors still seek to develop relations with international peacebuilders and donors. Yet, inequality and social exclusion (i.e. very high statistical indicators of poverty and inequality) are often little changed from the point at which a peace process began. This means that there has not been much of a peace dividend in everyday life (though there may have been a security dividend) in many conflict-affected societies.

Peace formation

It is widely accepted by archaeologists and anthropologists that peace systems emerge side by side with violence and war, and many of the innovations in the IPA have originally emerged from social sources. They may become locked into law, constitutions, doctrines, and practices at either state or international levels, one consolidating the other. Thus, social innovation has historically helped form peace, in turn shaping the state, regional, and international system. Trust networks, civil society, and social movements mobilize over issues pertaining to violence, inequality, identity, and unsustainability, which undermine peace and justice, thus renegotiating subsequent political order. Even with limited power and resources, extensive networks and grounded forms of legitimacy are the basis of peace formation. But this often represents an asymmetric challenge against political, economic, and military power.

Peace formation may draw on social, kin, and customary networks. It may include many different types of association, from unions to charities or regional trade networks. It may require formal international support for civil society. A rich web of relationships and networks is emerging from the local to the global that oppose embedded injustices and inequalities, encapsulated by the concept of global civil society. This operates transnationally and transversally (thus transcending traditional state boundaries and power structures through formal and informal networks) often with access to excellent scientific data as well as systems of political and social legitimacy. The capacity for self-organization for non-violent resistance or to provide support, public services, and even security and policing, where the state is non-existent or incapable, has been a common occurrence, as the case of Somalia has illustrated since the early 1990s. It is often aimed at providing public services—health, education, and basic security and needs—in an everyday setting. It may even play a role of organizing basic provisions, security, and services in everyday life during wartime, as has arisen during the desperate circumstances of the Syrian war. Yet, this phenomenon has limited capacity and is certainly no replaccment for a peace agreement, a well-ordered state, and stable regional order.

Basing peace projects on locally legitimate institutions, processes, customs, identities, and actors and their needs is vital for consensus and grounded legitimacy, however. Any such process will inevitably be a political choice, probably best made by a wide range of actors on the ground and enabled internationally. These processes blur the lines between formal and informal dynamics, the state, custom, and the traditional. Often women's groups are at the forefront, from Liberia to Bangladesh and Brazil. It places society, the village, the community, and the city at the centre of peace, rather than the state, security, and markets, and sheds light on the bottom-up dynamics necessary for the construction of a legitimate political order. It may utilize new forms of media and communications, not to mention transport and trade connections, or informal networks through academic or global social movements or INGOs. Without external support, of course, what such local mobilization can achieve in terms of peace formation may be very limited. Likewise, without local peace formation dynamics, international actors will probably be ineffective in promoting change or transformation, resulting in at best a negative hybrid form of peace where power is centralized and legitimacy is weak.

There were hints of peace formation in early post-Cold War peacebuilding frameworks. In post-war El Salvador UNESCO supported a Programme on 'Establishing a Culture of Peace' in 1992 that recognized that human development, poverty reduction, and addressing root causes also meant engaging with peace in cultural terms. By 1995, programmes were under way in Mozambique, Burundi, and the Philippines among other countries, to connect peacemaking with social values, assumptions, and historical perspectives and structures, eventually becoming part of a national culture. This approach was aimed at respect for difference, solidarity, and social justice in general, and the establishment of a wide range of venues and spaces of dialogue in which rights, representation, and justice might emerge. They would eventually coalesce into institutions, it was hoped. Local peace architectures link grass-roots organizations, local peace councils and committees, with local and national governmental institutions, as well as the international system more generally, notably its norms and institutional framework.

After the Lome Peace Accord in Sierra Leone in 1999, a Commission for the Consolidation of Peace was established along with national Commissions for Democracy, Human Rights, and others. The UN Peacebuilding Commission also helped to coordinate these. A parliamentary group also containing civil society members was established to work on a 'national peace infrastructure', which has included a range of fora, including a women's forum. Similarly, in Timor-Leste UNDP supported a Ministry of Peacebuilding's engagement with land and gender issues. Local peace councils of elders and activists became integrated into formal decentralized government as well as a National Peace Council, aimed at mediating conflict using local tools. Gradually the local structure built up into a national structure, with varying degrees of success. Nepal also established a Ministry of Peace and Reconstruction along similar lines, as did South Sudan.

In Somaliland in the early 1990s, localized peace agreements led by local elders utilizing customary law eventually resulted in a constitutional structure that included elected party representatives as well as a clan-oriented upper house. This grew out of widespread but localized peace conferences and discussions across Somaliland driven by the grass roots as well as business, clan, and political leaders, which has resulted in a reasonably stable polity, though it is as yet unrecognized as a state. Similarly, there was hope in Afghanistan, after 2001, that long-standing traditions of conflict resolution by tribal elders, village councils, the *jirga* dialogues, and the Peace

Shuras or Councils, at local, district, and national level might contribute to peace.

In Kenya after the post-election violence of 2007, an Open Forum was created and a Citizen's Agenda for Peace was developed. This was based on a peace movement started previously by a group of women in 1993, which led to the formation of a series of peace committees. This process drew in a number of ministries and levels of government and the media, and was also connected to the high-level peace process. Crucially, it was driven and legitimized by civil society aiming at substantial political reform, in a process that is still ongoing.

These innovations in civil society peacemaking have had varying degrees of success, mainly because of the asymmetric nature of their challenges against powerful actors and the degree of their international support. Better understanding of such local peace formation dynamics, which were significant for peace and reform for the state and the region, influenced the 2011 Busan Agreement on a 'New Deal for Engagement in Fragile States' amongst the main international donors. This emphasized the need for legitimate politics, people's security, and justice, drawing on the Millennium Development Goals (2000). The G7+ (an organization of so-called 'fragile states'—the 'club that everyone wants to leave'—including Timor-Leste, Somalia, Sierra Leone, and 15 others) influenced this agreement. Such developments brought to the fore the notion that societies build peace, not solely donors or state elites. This meant 'putting the last first' (an insight from Development Studies), which was also reflected in the UN and World Bank's report, *Pathways to Peace* (2017). The Sustainable Development Goals (2015) and the subsequent Sustaining Peace agenda (2017) further illustrated the close convergence of such practices, innovative research, and international policymaking on peace issues. Broadly speaking, insights of the various debates about peace and the IPA were now connected to wider questions about justice and sustainability.

Blockages to peace and counter-peace processes

Despite such progress, many peace processes have become frozen and open conflict has often restarted. The Russian regime's attack on Ukraine in 2022, coming long after the unsuccessful Minsk Agreements between the two countries in 2014, is one such example of why frozen or stalemated peace agreements can become so dangerous. Blockages in the peace process have commonly emerged across a wide range of cases over the last 30 years, where such agreements remain unimplemented or are impeded, often heralding a new war. Designing peace according to the needs, claims, and identities of the most marginalized and affected in conflict societies raises the age-old relationship between peace and power. Peace depends on the powerful laying down arms and power and agreeing to a compromise. Including social actors with little hard power is unlikely unless outside international actors, themselves with sufficient leverage, support peace formation and reject powerful elites' continuing control of politics. This is essentially what happened in the Northern Ireland conflict, where the EU and the USA made enormous efforts. Yet, elite actors, both domestic and international, control the levers and resources of the states system, and so have little incentive to support social claims, even if it offers longer-term legitimacy for a peace process. In Northern Ireland, in order to meet the multiple claims of the two main social groups, local elites as well as the British government had to accept a dilution of sovereignty and weakening of borders, as well as strengthening rights and the principle of equality. Despite this lesson, the tendency to connect any agreement and process to security, territorial sovereignty, and systems of power-sharing, however, has resulted in many contemporary frozen conflicts and peace processes.

Such problems are indicative of how blockages in a complex peace process emerge, often connected to polarized power structures connecting social groups with elites and international allies, or resting on contradictions between rights, identity, borders, and territorial control. Even more extreme is when they begin to add up to a parallel counter-peace framework. This represents a conservative tradition, concerned with preserving customs, territorial structures, centralized power, social, economic, and political stratifications, as well as balancing geopolitics. More authoritarian and illiberal forms of peace have emerged in examples such as Cambodia or Sri Lanka. Increasingly, an array of forces and actors have found ways of spoiling, blocking, and deflecting peace praxis, its liberal framework, and tendency to expand human rights into new terrains. Counter-peace strategies, following the logic of counter-revolution, operate to preserve privileges, power, and resources, often long held and thought to represent order. They have evolved to spoil and check peacekeeping, mediation, diplomacy, constitutional reform, human rights, economic redistribution, and equality. Violence remains proscribed but blockages lead to frozen conflicts and very lengthy peace engagements, as from the Golan Heights to Cyprus and the Balkans, which are always in danger of collapsing back into war—as in Ukraine in 2022.

Epilogue: new agendas for peace

The historical evolution of peace can be summarized as follows. The ancient to the medieval period saw the development of the victor's peace, wise governance to avoid war, truces and treaty-making to end wars, the realization of the advantages of achievement of prosperity, and a growing role for religious and social movements, which preached philosophical pluralism and pacifism.

The Enlightenment period added a concern with domestic and international law and norms to govern state behaviour, the liberal social contract (the constitutional peace), social movements for anti-slavery, enfranchisement, disarmament and pacifism, labour movements, human rights, and free trade.

The modern period saw these interests extend into social and gender issues, as well as equality and social justice (which is known as the civil peace). It also saw the emergence of international organizations, law, and conventions, forming an institutional peace. Other matters also emerged in the context of decolonization and the collapse of the Soviet Union, including self-determination, development, aid, the democratic peace, and trade. To achieve these, humanitarian intervention, liberal peacebuilding, and neoliberal statebuilding were developed, along with processes of transitional justice, in post-conflict countries around the world. Over time all of these developments coalesced into an international peace architecture, complex and fragmentary, but significant nonetheless.

With the notable return of authoritarian nationalism, with Russia's war in Ukraine in 2022, Russia's apparent alliance with China and other regional powers, and nationalist ideologies competing with Western versions of liberal peace, there is also a major question as to what version of peace and international order the global south might prefer. Will such states opt for a victor's peace and realpolitik all over again, will new alternatives emerge, and would they be built on the existing international peace architecture?

New agendas and the IPA

The older notions of peace still play an important role as foundational layers of the IPA. Peacemaking and the complex machinery it requires has advanced considerably throughout history, even though it remains far from ideal. When confronted with transnational problems and political tensions which relate to inequality, environmental unsustainability, injustice, the arms trade, human trafficking, nuclear proliferation, urban conflict, and the use of new technologies, new agendas for peace are emerging. As peace systems have become more complex, with new layers and tools being added as conflict, violence, and war evolve, they have also become more costly and require more political will.

The evolution of the IPA has brought together the victor's peace applied to imperial and industrial state orders in stage one, which remains relevant in policy thinking and influences conflict management approaches. Stage two, the constitutional and liberal peace, were significant attempts to move beyond the cruder versions of the victor's peace, by focusing on democracy, human rights, development, and free trade, and placing the West as the leader of the IPA. This has provided the basis for the bulk of post-Enlightenment advances in peace thinking and practices.

Similarly, the third strand of the IPA, which dealt with expanded (ECOSOC) rights after industrialized warfare ended in 1945, and decolonization thereafter, was also influential. This is now the goal of much of the UN system, and represents the main contribution of the 20th century, being consolidated in stage four, the liberal peacebuilding system, after the end of the Cold War.

The four components of the liberal peace—victor's, constitutional, institutional, and civil peace, as well as the first, second, and third generation approaches to peacemaking—depend upon a mix of external actors' intervention, local agency, and legitimacy. The liberal peace is depicted in Figure 10 and the first three generations of peacemaking can be summarized as in Figure 11.

10. A genealogy of the liberal peace.

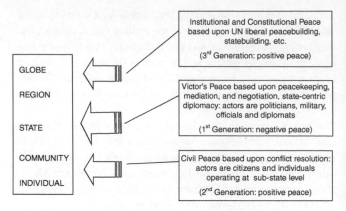

GLOBE

REGION

STATE

COMMUNITY

INDIVIDUAL

Institutional and Constitutional Peace based upon UN liberal peacebuilding, statebuilding, etc.

(3rd Generation: positive peace)

Victor's Peace based upon peacekeeping, mediation, and negotiation, state-centric diplomacy: actors are politicians, military, officials and diplomats

(1st Generation: negative peace)

Civil Peace based upon conflict resolution: actors are citizens and individuals operating at sub-state level

(2nd Generation: positive peace)

11. **Three generations of approaches to peacemaking.**

However, after failures from Somalia to Rwanda and the Balkans, the IPA began to shift into a more limited neoliberal framework for peace in stage five as was applied in Afghanistan and Iraq. Given the failures in the 2010s and onwards in Libya, Syria, Yemen, Afghanistan, and other cases, stage six is as yet undetermined. It must stabilize many frozen conflicts and open wars, from Syria to Ukraine, as well as deal with new phenomena and technologies in warfare (AI and automated weapons, proliferation of small arms and worse, hybrid warfare, urban violence, and more), as well as nationalism, populism, inequality, authoritarianism, and environmental unsustainability.

A new layer of the IPA is now required to deal with new conflict dynamics and the demands for a form of peace more closely connected with justice. This process will probably not lead to a world government (to the disappointment of some liberal internationalists and the relief of others attuned to nationalism, political, and identity differences), however, but instead may indicate a world community made up of interlocking, pluralist, or 'pluriversal' 'peaces': a 'Grand Design' to quote the Duc de Sully (1560–1641), a 17th-century philosopher. It may include different types of states, institutions, and norms, as well as new transnational and transversal networks that include official, civil, and social actors and groups. It reaffirms that only cooperation, inclusivity, pluralism, and redistribution can maintain an ever-evolving IPA. The UNESCO definition of a 'culture of peace' (cited above) represents a sophisticated institutional understanding of peace. The more recent Sustaining Peace agenda the UN is developing (2018) connects such thinking to political, diplomatic, military, and economic tools, in the broader context of justice and sustainability issues, which is a further step forward. Yet, as the World Bank has estimated, 1.5 billion people are still affected by conflict.

A new layer of the IPA and generation of peace thinking and practice may involve hybrid, empathetic, emancipatory notions of peace resting upon pluralism and international responses to inequality, meaning local and global redistribution, sustainability and global justice, the recognition of a range of everyday and transnational peace agencies, and participatory forms of democracy from the local to the global. Rather than being externally imposed it might form locally and be *enabled* in multiple ways by a range of international and local actors cooperating with each other (as with the local infrastructures for peace already mentioned). It requires historical, distributive, and global justice.

Overall, the IPA represents a response to past conflicts and to prevent future conflict. It has often reflected the interests and ideologies of dominant actors in the international system. Even so, as this volume has illustrated, approaches to peace are developing quickly and with far-reaching effects for improving everyday lives for humanity. Much more remains to be done, however.

The outcome of the rich, global, historical heritage of peace thinking and peacemaking spanning the arts to history and politics, as well as social struggles for equality outlined in this short study, is the emergence of interconnected and multiple forms of peace. Its culmination lies in a general recognition that the vast majority of humanity have preferred, and actively worked towards, a culture of peace. Many have worked for this selflessly throughout human history, across all fields of human knowledge, leaving an inestimable legacy upon which future generations can continue to build.

Further reading

Chapter 2: Defining peace

Augustine, *The City of God against the Pagans*, trans. R. W. Dyson (New York: Cambridge University Press, 1998).

Confucius, *Confucius: Analects—With Selections from Traditional Commentaries* (c.551–479 BC), trans. E. Slingerland (Indianapolis: Hackett Publishing, 2003).

Doyle, Michael, 'Kant, Liberal Legacies, and Foreign Affairs', *Philosophy and Public Affairs*, 12 (1983).

Erasmus, *'The Complaint of Peace', The Essential Erasmus*, ed. John Dolan (New York: Continuum, 1990).

Foucault, M., 'Truth and Power', in P. Rabinow (ed.), *The Foucault Reader* (London: Penguin, 1989).

Gallie, W. B., *Philosophers of Peace and War: Kant, Clausewitz, Marx, Engels and Tolstoy* (Cambridge: Cambridge University Press, 1978).

Gandhi, Mahatma, *The Collected Works of Mahatma Gandhi* (New Delhi: Publications Division, Ministry of Information and Broadcasting, Govt. of India, 1994).

Gittings, John, *The Glorious Art of Peace* (Oxford: Oxford University Press, 2012).

Hinsley, F. H., *Power and the Pursuit of Peace* (Cambridge: Cambridge University Press, 1963).

Hobbes, Thomas, *Leviathan* (Oxford: Oxford University Press, 1998 [1651]).

Howard, Michael, *The Invention of Peace and War* (London: Profile Books, 2000).

Kant, Immanuel, *Perpetual Peace* (London: Allen and Unwin, 1917 [1795]).

Kelly, Raymond, *Warless Societies and the Origin of War* (Ann Arbor, Mich.: University of Michigan Press, 2000).

Kissinger, H., *A World Restored: Metternich, Castlereagh and the Problems of Peace, 1812–22* (Boston: Houghton Mifflin, 1957).

Sully, Duc de, *Sully's Grand Design of Henry IV: From the Memoirs of Maximilien De Béthune* (Wentworth Press, 2016 [1638/1662]).

UN Report of the Secretary-General, 'Peacebuilding and sustaining peace', A/72/707–S/2018/43, 18 January 2018, para. 6.

<http://www.peacefulsocieties.org/>.

Chapter 3: The victor's peace in history

Galtung, J., 'Violence, Peace, and Peace Research', *Journal of Peace Research*, 6:3 (1969).

Hammarskjöld, Dag, *Summary Study*, UN doc. A/3943, 9 October 1958.

Hegel, G. W. F., *Philosophy of Right* (London: Prometheus, 1996).

Hobbes, Thomas, *Leviathan* (Oxford: Oxford University Press, 1998 [1651]).

Keynes, J. M., *The Economic Consequences of the Peace* (London: Macmillan, 1920).

Kissinger, Henry, *A World Restored: Metternich, Castlereagh and the Problems of Peace, 1812–22* (Boston: Houghton Mifflin, 1957).

Machiavelli, Niccolò, *The Prince*, trans. Harvey Mansfield (Chicago: University of Chicago Press, 1985).

Princen, Thomas, *Intermediaries in International Conflict* (Princeton: Princeton University Press, 1992).

Sherman, W. H., *John Dee: The Politics of History in the English Renaissance* (Amherst, Mass.: Massachusetts University Press, 1995).

Sun Tzu, *The Art of War*, trans. John Minford (New York: Viking, 2002).

Thucydides, *The Peloponnesian War*, trans. Steven Lattimore (Indianapolis: Hackett, 1998).

Vitoria, Francisco, *The Law of War on the Indians*, trans. Ernest Nys (London: Oceana Publications Inc., 1964 [1532]).

Chapter 4: Peace in history: towards the Enlightenment

Cruce, Emerie, *The New Cyneas of Emerie Cruce*, trans. Thomas Willing Balch (Charleston, SC: BiblioLife, 2009 [1623]).

Erasmus, 'The Arts of Peace', in Lisa Jardine (ed.), *The Education of a Christian Prince* (Cambridge: Cambridge University Press, 1997 [1516]).

Erasmus, 'Antipolemus, or, the Plea of Reason, Religion, and Humanity against War', reprinted in *The Book of Peace: A Collection of Essays on War and Peace* (Boston: George C. Beckwith, 1845).

Fry, Douglas, *Beyond War* (Oxford: Oxford University Press, 2007).

Grotius, Hugo, *The Rights of War and Peace*, trans. A. C. Campbell (London: Dunne, 1901 [1625]).

Holt, J. C., *Magna Carta* (2nd edn Cambridge: Cambridge University Press, 1992).

Johansen, B., *Native American Legal Tradition* (New York: Greenwood, 1998).

Kant, Immanuel, *Perpetual Peace* (London: Allen and Unwin, 1917 [1795]).

Locke, John, *A Letter Concerning Toleration*, and *Two Treatises on Government*, ed. Ian Shapiro (New Haven: Yale University Press, 2003).

Marx, Karl, and Engels, Friedrich, *The Communist Manifesto* (London: Penguin, 2006 [1848]).

Penn, William, 'An Essay towards the Present and Future Peace of Europe', in *The Peace of Europe* (London: Everyman, 1993 [1693]).

Rousseau, Jean-Jacques, *The Social Contract*, ed. G. D. Cole (Thousand Oaks, Calif.: BN Publishers, 2007 [1762]).

Thoreau, Henry David, *Resistance to Civil Government* (Carlisle, Mass.: Applewood Books, 2000 [1849]).

Tolstoy, Leo, *The Kingdom of God is Within You* (Lincoln, Nebr.: Bison Books, 1984 [1894]).

Chapter 5: Peace in modernity: the constitutional peace

Bentham, J., *The Collected Works* (Oxford: Clarendon, 1996 [1839]).

Ceadel, Martin, *Thinking About Peace and War* (Oxford: Oxford University Press, 1987).

Doyle, Michael, 'Kant, Liberal Legacies, and Foreign Affairs', *Philosophy and Public Affairs*, 12 (1983).

Gittings, John, *The Glorious Art of Peace* (Oxford: Oxford University Press, 2012).

Kant, Immanuel, *Perpetual Peace* (London: Allen and Unwin, 1917 [1795]).

Locke, John, *A Letter Concerning Toleration*, and *Two Treaties on Government*, ed. Ian Shapiro (New Haven: Yale University Press, 2003).

Mill, John Stuart, *On Liberty* (Oxford: Oxford University Press, 1998 [1859]).

Mill, John Stuart, *Principles of Political Economy* (Oxford: Oxford University Press, 2010 [1848]).

Paris, Roland, and Sisk, Timothy, *The Dilemmas of Statebuilding* (London: Routledge, 2008).

Ricardo, David, *On the Principles of Political Economy and Taxation* (Amherst, Mass.: Prometheus Books, 1996 [1821]).

Roberts, Adam, and Kingsbury, Benedict (eds), *United Nations, Divided World* (2nd edn London: Oxford University Press, 1996).

Smith, Adam, *An Inquiry into the Nature and Causes of the Wealth of Nations* (Chicago: University of Chicago Press; Facsimile of 1904 edition, 1977 [1776]).

Chapter 6: The next step: an institutional peace

Barash, David, *Approaches to Peace* (Oxford: Oxford University Press, 2000).

Brownlie, Ian, *Principles of Public International Law* (Oxford: Oxford University Press, 2008).

Carr, E. H., *The Twenty Years Crisis* (London: Macmillan, 1939).

Fanon, F., *The Wretched of the Earth*, trans. Constance Farrington (New York: Grove Weidenfeld, [1961] 1963).

Geneva Conventions, 1864, 1949, and *Additional Protocols*, 1977.

Gittings, John, *The Glorious Art of Peace* (Oxford: Oxford University Press, 2012).

Ikenberry, G. John, *After Victory* (Princeton: Princeton University Press, 2001).

'International Covenant on Economic, Social and Cultural Rights', *General Assembly Resolution 2200A (XXI)*, 16 December 1966 (entered into force 3 January 1976, in accordance with article 27).

Keynes, John Maynard, *The Economic Consequences of the Peace* (London: Macmillan, 1920).

Link, Arthur S., et al. (eds), *The Papers of Woodrow Wilson*, xli: *January 24–April 6, 1917* (Princeton: Princeton University Press, 1983).

Macmillan, Margaret, *The Peacemakers* (London: John Murray, 2003).

Mitrany, David, *The Functional Theory of Politics* (London: Martin Robertson, 1975).

Owen, Nicolas (ed.), *Human Rights, Human Wrongs* (Oxford: Oxford University Press, 2002).

Penn, William, 'An Essay towards the Present and Future Peace of Europe', in *The Peace of Europe* (London: Everyman, 1993 [1693]).

Rieff, David, *A Bed for the Night* (London: Vintage, 2002).

Saint-Pierre, Abbé de, *A Project for Settling an Everlasting Peace in Europe, 1714–1738* (London, 1714).

Steel, R., *Walter Lippmann and the American Century* (Boston: Little Brown and Company, 1980).

Taylor, Paul, and Groom, A. J. R. (eds), *The UN at the Millennium* (London: Continuum, 2000).

Williams, Andrew, *Failed Imagination: New World Orders of the Twentieth Century* (Manchester: Manchester University Press, 1998).

Chapter 7: A radical phase: a civil peace and social advocacy

Anderson, Mary B., *Do No Harm* (Boulder, Colo.: Lynne Rienner Publishers, 1999).

Azar, E. A., *The Management of Protracted Social Conflict* (London: Dartmouth Publishing, 1990).

Barash, David, *Approaches to Peace* (Oxford: Oxford University Press, 2000).

Boulding, Elise, *Cultures of Peace* (Syracuse, NY: Syracuse University Press, 2000).

Einstein, Albert, Freud, Sigmund, and Jäckh, Ernst, *Why War? 'Open Letters' Between Einstein & Freud* (London: The New Commonwealth. A society for the promotion of international law and order, 1934).

Fanon, F., *The Wretched of the Earth*, trans. Constance Farrington (New York: Grove Weidenfeld, 1963 [1961]).

Foucault, M., *The Birth of Politics*, trans. Graham Burchell (London: Palgrave, 2009).

Freire, P., *Pedagogy of the Oppressed* (London: Penguin, 1996 [1970]).

Hochschild, Adam, *Bury the Chains* (London: Macmillan, 2005).

Josselin, Daphne, and Wallace, William (eds), *Non-State Actors in World Politics* (London: Palgrave, 2001).

Keane, John, *Global Civil Society?* (Cambridge: Cambridge University Press, 2003).

Keck, Margeret E., and Sikkind, Kathryn, *Activists Beyond Borders* (Ithaca, NY: Cornell University Press, 1998).

Mendlovitz, S., and Walker, R. B. J. (eds), *Towards a Just World Peace* (London: Butterworths, 1987).

Ramsbotham, Oliver, and Woodhouse, Tom, *Humanitarian Intervention in Contemporary Conflict* (Cambridge: Polity Press, 2005).

Russell, Bertrand, *The Collected Papers of Bertrand Russell*, xiv: *Pacifism and Revolution 1916–18* (London: Unwin Hyman, 1995).

Scott, J. C., *Domination and the Arts of Resistance* (New Haven: Yale University Press, 1990).

Sen, Amartya, *Development as Freedom* (Oxford: Oxford University Press, 1999).

Tadjbakhsh, Sharhbanou, and Chenoy, Anuradha M., *Human Security: Concepts and Implications* (London: Routledge, 2006).

Willets, Peter, 'From "Consultative Arrangements" to "Partnership": The Changing Status of NGOs in Diplomacy at the UN', *Global Governance*, 6 (2000).

Chapter 8: The development of an international peace architecture

Bellamy, Alex, and Williams, Paul, 'Peace Operations and Global Order', *International Peacekeeping*, 10:4 (2004).

Boutros-Ghali, Boutros, *An Agenda for Peace: Preventative Diplomacy, Peacemaking and Peacekeeping* (New York: United Nations, 1992).

Burton, J., *World Society* (Cambridge: Cambridge University Press, 1972).

Busan Partnership for Effective Development Co-operation. Fourth High Level Forum on Aid Effectiveness (Busan, Republic of Korea, 29 November–1 December 2011).

Doyle, Michael W., 'Liberalism and World Politics', *The American Political Science Review*, 80:4 (December 1986): 1151–69.

Hinsley, F. H., *Power and the Pursuit of Peace* (Cambridge: Cambridge University Press, 1963).

Mitrany, D. A., *The Functional Theory of Politics* (London: Martin Robertson, 1975).

Richmond, Oliver P., *Maintaining Order, Making Peace* (London: Palgrave, 2002).

Richmond, Oliver P., *The Transformation of Peace* (London: Palgrave, 2005).

Richmond, Oliver P., *The Grand Design* (Oxford: Oxford University Press, 2021).

Tuck, Richard, *The Rights of War and Peace* (Oxford: Oxford University Press, 1999).

UNDP, *Human Development Report* (New York: UNDP, 2020).

UN General Assembly (2015) 'Sustainable Development Goals (SDGs), 2030 Agenda for Sustainable Development', *A/RES/70/1*, adopted by UN GA, September 2015.

UN Secretary-General, 'Report of the Secretary-General, Peacebuilding and Sustaining Peace', *A/72/707–S/2018/43* (New York: United Nations, 2018).

Chapter 9: Peacekeeping, peacebuilding, and statebuilding

Azar, E. A., *The Management of Protracted Social Conflict* (London: Dartmouth Publishing, 1990).

Bercovitch, J. (ed.), *Resolving International Conflicts: The Theory and Practice of Mediation* (London: Boulder, 1996).

Call, Charles T., and Cook, Susan E., 'On Democratisation and Peacebuilding', *Global Governance*, 9:2 (2003).

Cousens, Elizabeth, and Kumar, C., *Peacebuilding as Politics* (Boulder, Colo.: Lynne Rienner, 2001).

Fukuyama, Francis, *State Building: Governance and Order in the Twenty First Century* (London: Profile, 2004).

International Commission on Intervention, *The Responsibility to Protect: The Report of the International Commission on Intervention and State Sovereignty* (Ottawa: International Development Research Centre, 2002).

Kapur, D., 'The State in a Changing World: A Critique of the 1997 World Development Report', *WCFIA Working Paper No. 98–02* (1998).

Lederach, Jean Paul, *Building Peace* (Washington, DC: United States Institute of Peace, 1997).

Lund, Michael S., *Preventing Violent Conflicts* (Washington, DC: USIP, 1996).

Miall, Hugh, *Conflict Transformation: A Multi-Dimensional Task* (Berghof Handbook for Conflict Transformation, 2004).

Peacebuilding & The United Nations (United Nations Peacebuilding Support Office, United Nations, 2012).

Richmond, Oliver P., and Franks, Jason, *Liberal Peace Transitions: Between Statebuilding and Peacebuilding* (Edinburgh: Edinburgh University Press, 2009).

Schmid, Herman, 'Peace Research and Politics', *Journal of Peace Research*, 5:3 (1968).

UN General Assembly Resolution 60/180 (20 December 2005).

UN Secretary Report on 'Peacebuilding in the Immediate Aftermath of Conflict', A/63/881 (11 June 2009).

Wilkinson, Richard, and Pickett, Kate, *The Spirit Level: Why Equality Is Better for Everyone* (London: Penguin, 2009).

World Bank, *The State in a Changing World* (Washington, DC: World Bank, 1997).

Zartman, I. William, *Ripe for Resolution* (Oxford: For the Council of Foreign Relations, 1989).

Chapter 10: Hybrid forms of peace, peace formation, and counter-peace

Alden, C., 'The United Nations and Demilitarisation in Mozambique', *International Peacekeeping*, 2:2 (1995).

Bhabha, H., *The Location of Culture* (London: Routledge, 1994).

Boege, Volker, Brown, Anne, Clements, Kevin P., and Nolan, Anna, 'States Emerging from Hybrid Political Orders—Pacific Experiences', *The Australian Centre for Peace and Conflict Studies (ACPACS) Occasional Papers Series* (2008).

Brown, Anne, *Security and Development in the Pacific Islands* (Boulder, Colo.: Lynne Rienner, 2007).

Chambers, R., *Rural Development: Putting the Last First* (London: Longman, 1983).

G7+, *Dili Declaration*, April 2010: 'Busan Partnership for Effective Development Co-operation', *Fourth High Level Forum On Aid Effectiveness* (Busan, Republic of Korea, 29 November–1 December 2011).

Hadjipavlou, M., 'The Cyprus Conflict: Root Causes and Implications for Peacebuilding', *Journal of Peace Research*, 44:3 (2007).

Hayman, C., 'Ripples into Waves: Locally Led Peacebuilding on a National Scale' (Peace Direct/Quakers UN Office, 2010).

Home for Cooperation, <https://www.home4cooperation.info/>.

Ihsanoglu, E., Allen Nan, Susan, Cherian Mampilly, Zachariah, and Bartoli, Andrea, *Peacemaking: From Practice to Theory* (Westport, Conn.: Praeger, 2011).

Jonas, Susanne, *Of Centaurs and Doves: Guatemala's Peace Process* (Boulder, Colo.: Westview Press, 2000).

Kemp, Graham, and Fry, Douglas P., *Keeping the Peace: Peaceful Societies Around the World* (London: Routledge, 2004).

Lister, Sarah, 'Understanding State-Building and Local Government in Afghanistan', *Crisis States Research Centre Working Paper No. 14* (May 2007).

National Peace Council <https://www.peace-srilanka.org/>.

Pouligny, B., *Peace Operations Seen from Below* (London: Hurst, 2006).

Report of the Secretary-General, 'Peacebuilding and Sustaining Peace', *A/72/707–S/2018/43*, 18 January 2018, para. 6.

Richmond, Oliver P., *A Post-Liberal Peace* (London: Routledge, 2011).

Roberts, Adam, and Garton Ash, Timothy (eds), *Civil Resistance and Power Politics* (Oxford: Oxford University Press, 2009).

UNDP, *Governance for Peace* (New York, 2012).

UNESCO, Culture of Peace Programme in El Salvador (1992).

UN Secretary General Report on 'Peacebuilding in the Immediate Aftermath of Conflict', A/63/881 (11 June 2009).

World Bank, *Issues and Options for Improving Engagement between the World Bank and Civil Society Organisations* (Washington, DC, 2005).

Wyeth, V., 'Knights in Fragile Armour: The Rise of the G7+', *Global Governance*, 18 (2011).

Index

Peace

Peace

Peace

USA 30, 63, 64, 72, 80, 82, 89, 92,
    96, 106, 121

V

Vitoria, Francisco de 36

W

war crimes 64
War Guilt Clause 56
War on Terror 92, 107
Weber, Max 11
Wells, H. G. 51, 82
welfare 38, 46, 64, 81, 86, 89, 101,
    105, 107, 115
West, the 6, 10, 12, 18, 22, 58, 60,
    64, 67, 79, 81, 82, 84, 85, 86,
    88, 89, 105, 106, 109, 124, 125
  non-West 5, 106

Westphalia 9, 30, 40, 41,
    44, 53
Wilson, President Woodrow 27,
    55–6, 80
women's groups 90, 118
World Bank 11, 47, 76, 89, 92, 101,
    105, 107, 108, 127
World Disarmament
    Conference 81
world government 2, 36, 50–3,
    65, 79, 82

Y

Yemen 2
Yugoslavia 28, 73, 85

Z

Zartman, William 96

Peace

DIPLOMACY
A Very Short Introduction
Joseph M. Siracusa

Like making war, diplomacy has been around a very long time, at least since the Bronze Age. It was primitive by today's standards, there were few rules, but it was a recognizable form of diplomacy. Since then, diplomacy has evolved greatly, coming to mean different things, to different persons, at different times, ranging from the elegant to the inelegant. Whatever one's definition, few could doubt that the course and consequences of the major events of modern international diplomacy have shaped and changed the global world in which we live. Joseph M. Siracusa introduces the subject of diplomacy from a historical perspective, providing examples from significant historical phases and episodes to illustrate the art of diplomacy in action.

'Professor Siracusa provides a lively introduction to diplomacy through the perspective of history.'

Gerry Woodard, Senior Fellow in Political Science at the University of Melbourne and former Australasian Ambassador in Asia

www.oup.com/vsi

HUMAN RIGHTS
A Very Short Introduction
Andrew Clapham

An appeal to human rights in the face of injustice can be a heartfelt and morally justified demand for some, while for others it remains merely an empty slogan. Taking an international perspective and focusing on highly topical issues such as torture, arbitrary detention, privacy, health and discrimination, this *Very Short Introduction* will help readers to understand for themselves the controversies and complexities behind this vitally relevant issue. Looking at the philosophical justification for rights, the historical origins of human rights and how they are formed in law, Andrew Clapham explains what our human rights actually are, what they might be, and where the human rights movement is heading.

www.oup.com/vsi

THE UNITED NATIONS
A Very Short Introduction
Jussi M. Hanhimäki

With this much-needed introduction to the UN, Jussi Hanhimäki
engages the current debate over the organization's effectiveness
as he provides a clear understanding of how it was originally
conceived, how it has come to its present form, and how it
must confront new challenges in a rapidly changing world. After
a brief history of the United Nations and its predecessor, the
League of Nations, the author examines the UN's successes
and failures as a guardian of international peace and security,
as a promoter of human rights, as a protector of international law,
and as an engineer of socio-economic development.

www.oup.com/vsi

INTERNATIONAL RELATIONS
A Very Short Introduction
Paul Wilkinson

Of undoubtable relevance today, in a post-9-11 world of growing political tension and unease, this *Very Short Introduction* covers the topics essential to an understanding of modern international relations. Paul Wilkinson explains the theories and the practice that underlies the subject, and investigates issues ranging from foreign policy, arms control, and terrorism, to the environment and world poverty. He examines the role of organizations such as the United Nations and the European Union, as well as the influence of ethnic and religious movements and terrorist groups which also play a role in shaping the way states and governments interact. This up-to-date book is required reading for those seeking a new perspective to help untangle and decipher international events.

www.oup.com/vsi

THE EUROPEAN UNION
A Very Short Introduction
John Pinder & Simon Usherwood

This *Very Short Introduction* explains the European Union in plain English. Fully updated for 2007 to include controversial and current topics such as the Euro currency, the EU's enlargement, and its role in ongoing world affairs, this accessible guide shows how and why the EU has developed from 1950 to the present. Covering a range of topics from the Union's early history and the ongoing interplay between 'eurosceptics' and federalists, to the single market, agriculture, and the environment, the authors examine the successes and failures of the EU, and explain the choices that lie ahead in the 21st century.

THE U.S CONGRESS
A Very Short Introduction
Donald Richie

The world's most powerful national legislature, the U. S. Congress, remains hazy as an institution. This *Very Short Introduction* to Congress highlights the rules, precedents, and practices of the Senate and House of Representatives, and offers glimpses into their committees and floor proceedings to reveal the complex processes by which they enact legislation. In *The U.S. Congress*, Donald A. Ritchie, a congressional historian for more than thirty years, takes readers on a fascinating, behind-the-scenes tour of Capitol Hill-pointing out the key players, explaining their behaviour, and translating parliamentary language into plain English.

www.oup.com/vsi

FREE SPEECH
A Very Short Introduction
Nigel Warburton

'I disapprove of what you say, but I will defend to the death your right to say it' This slogan, attributed to Voltaire, is frequently quoted by defenders of free speech. Yet it is rare to find anyone prepared to defend all expression in every circumstance, especially if the views expressed incite violence. So where do the limits lie? What is the real value of free speech? Here, Nigel Warburton offers a concise guide to important questions facing modern society about the value and limits of free speech: Where should a civilized society draw the line? Should we be free to offend other people's religion? Are there good grounds for censoring pornography? Has the Internet changed everything? This Very Short Introduction is a thought-provoking, accessible, and up-to-date examination of the liberal assumption that free speech is worth preserving at any cost.

'The genius of Nigel Warburton's *Free Speech* lies not only in its extraordinary clarity and incisiveness. Just as important is the way Warburton addresses freedom of speech - and attempts to stifle it - as an issue for the 21st century. More than ever, we need this book.'

Denis Dutton, University of Canterbury, New Zealand

www.oup.com/vsi

CITIZENSHIP
A Very Short Introduction
Richard Bellamy

Interest in citizenship has never been higher. But what does it mean to be a citizen of a modern, complex community? Why is citizenship important? Can we create citizenship, and can we test for it? In this fascinating Very Short Introduction, Richard Bellamy explores the answers to these questions and more in a clear and accessible way. He approaches the subject from a political perspective, to address the complexities behind the major topical issues. Discussing the main models of citizenship, exploring how ideas of citizenship have changed through time from ancient Greece to the present, and examining notions of rights and democracy, he reveals the irreducibly political nature of citizenship today.

'Citizenship is a vast subject for a short introduction, but Richard Bellamy has risen to the challenge with aplomb.'

Mark Garnett, TLS

www.oup.com/vsi

AMERICAN POLITICAL PARTIES AND ELECTIONS
A Very Short Introduction
Sandy L. Maisel

Few Americans and even fewer citizens of other nations understand the electoral process in the United States. Still fewer understand the role played by political parties in the electoral process or the ironies within the system. Participation in elections in the United States is much lower than in the vast majority of mature democracies. Perhaps this is because of the lack of competition in a country where only two parties have a true chance of winning, despite the fact that a large number of citizens claim allegiance to neither and think badly of both. Studying these factors, you begin to get a very clear picture indeed of the problems that underlay this much trumpeted electoral system.

PRIVACY
A Very Short Introduction
Raymond Wacks

Professor Raymond Wacks is a leading international expert on privacy. For more than three decades he has published numerous books and articles on this controversial subject. Privacy is a fundamental value that is under attack from several quarters. Electronic surveillance, biometrics, CCTV, ID cards, RFID codes, online security, the monitoring of employees, the uses and misuses of DNA, - to name but a few - all raise fundamental questions about our right to privacy. This *Very Short Introduction* also analyzes the tension between free speech and privacy generated by intrusive journalism, photography, and gratuitous disclosures by the media of the private lives of celebrities. Professor Wacks concludes this stimulating introduction by considering the future of privacy in our society.